New Ways in Teaching Young Children

Linda Schinke-Llano and Rebecca Rauff,
Editors

New Ways in TESOL Series

Innovative Classroom Techniques

Jack C. Richards, Series Editor

Teachers of English to Speakers of Other Languages, Inc.

Typeset in Garamond Book and Tiffany Demi
by Capitol Communication Systems, Inc., Crofton, Maryland USA
and printed by
Pantagraph Printing, Bloomington, Illinois USA

Teachers of English to Speakers of Other Languages, Inc.
1600 Cameron Street, Suite 300
Alexandria, VA 22314 USA
Tel 703-836-0774 • Fax 703-836-7864

Director of Communications and Marketing: Helen Kornblum
Senior Editor: Marilyn Kupetz
Copy Editor: Ellen Garshick
Cover Design and Spot Art: Ann Kammerer

Every effort has been made to contact the copyright holders for permission to reprint borrowed material. We regret any oversights that may have occurred and will rectify them in future printings of this work.

TESOL thanks Mary Agnes Garman, the staff, and the students of Kings Park Elementary School, Burke, Virginia, for their participation and assistance.

ISBN 0-939791-63-3
Library of Congress Catalogue No. 95-062078

To children everywhere . . .

Contents

Acknowledgments

We would like to thank Jack Richards, Series Editor, for the opportunity to edit this volume; Helen Kornblum and Marilyn Kupetz of the TESOL Central Office for their patience and professionalism; Ellen Garshick for her insightful editorial assistance; and, most of all, our TESOL colleagues around the world who took time from teaching young children to share their ideas. Finally, we thank our respective families, Frank and Melissa Llano and Jim and Andy Rauff, for their support of all our endeavors.

Introduction

Teaching English as a second or foreign language to young children offers special challenges. Like their older counterparts, young L2 learners may vary greatly in their aptitude for L2 learning, their motivation for the experience, and their interest in language learning in general and in individual language activities. Unlike the majority of their older counterparts, however, younger learners may also be experiencing their first encounter with formal education. Thus, teachers of young learners must often address areas of learning taken for granted by those who teach older learners.

Specifically, in addition to imparting English skills, teachers of children must foster socialization; heighten an awareness of the self, the immediate classroom community, and the community beyond the walls of the school; introduce students to content concepts; and begin to expose students to various media of communication—art, drama, literature, and music. As if these goals were not daunting enough, teachers must accomplish them through activities that are appropriate for both the chronological age and the cognitive development of the students and that hold their attention. In short, teachers of young children must address the whole child—the child's physical, cognitive, social, and emotional aspects—with activities that are enjoyable.

The contents of this volume demonstrate that the contributors are clearly aware of their multiple roles in teaching children. Each activity is a language activity, yet its aim—whether pronunciation practice, vocabulary development, or concept development—is embedded in a format that creatively achieves other goals as well. Thus, rather than categorizing the activities in this volume in the traditional listening/speaking/reading/ writing schema, we present them in 14 categories that illustrate the creativity and diversity involved in teaching ESL/EFL to young children.

Part I, Social Interaction, includes activities that range from first-time classroom encounters to learning about and working with special-needs children. In Real-Life Situations (Part II), activities address skills needed beyond the classroom. Activities in The Senses (Part III) heighten students' self-awareness as well as their awareness of their relationship to the world. Activities grouped under Learning Through Actions (Part IV) acknowledge the unique role that physical activity can play in reinforcing learning for children. Realia (Part V) increases students' attention to the physical characteristics of objects around them. Parts VI–X, Literature, Art, Music, Drama, and Storytelling, demonstrate ways to enhance learning through the rich variety of forms people use to express themselves. Writing (Part XI) offers activities that range from forming sentences to creating a school newspaper. Content Areas (Part XII) recognizes the role of ESL/EFL teachers in teaching or reinforcing content knowledge. Finally, the two sections on games, Dice and Board Games (Part XIII) and Card and Other Games (Part XIV), demonstrate that purposeful language lessons can be framed in activities that appear to be solely entertainment.

Although teaching English as a second or foreign language to children offers special challenges, every teacher engaged in this process knows that it offers special rewards as well. The joy of watching young children progress—not only linguistically, but also cognitively, socially, and emotionally—is unequaled. Just as the activities contributed to this volume recognize the multiple roles of teachers, they also convey the contributors' enthusiasm for and joy in teaching young children. Readers of this volume and their students will surely benefit from these purposeful, creative, and enjoyable activities that are the hallmark of those who teach English to young children.

Users' Guide to Activities

Part XIV: Card and Other Games

Part I: Social Interaction

Left to right: David Ha and Steve Amuz at Kings Park Elementary School, Burke, Virginia, USA.

Matching Pictures

Levels
Intermediate

Aims
Practice the language of description
Review colors and adjectives

Class Time
15-20 minutes

Resources
Pairs of identical pictures (e.g., children, animals, birds, houses, cars)—one picture per child

Procedure

1. Give each child one picture. Ask the children to study their pictures closely and think about how they would describe them to someone.
2. Tell the children to put their pictures facedown on their desks, move around the class, and try to find the child who has a picture that matches theirs by describing their pictures to each other. For example,

   A: My picture is a big black dog.
   B: My picture is a small brown dog.

3. When two students with matching pictures find each other, have them check by comparing their pictures and sit down if they are right. The first pair to sit down are the winners, but the game continues until all the children have matched their pictures.

Caveats and Options

For more advanced students, select pictures that are more detailed (e.g., a big black dog seated under an apple tree).

Ronald Jackup is a freelance EFL teacher and writer.

Contributor

Stamping Out Insults

Levels
High beginning

Aims
Discuss why people
insult others
Learn kind words and
be encouraged to use
them

Class Time
2 hours

Resources
Colored markers
Scissors
Poster board
Colored construction
paper
Glue or tape

Procedure

1. As a class, discuss insults—what they are, why people use them, and how they make others feel. Discuss why some groups in society are particular targets of insults. An appropriate story, a news event, or an actual situation from the students' lives can help provide context for the discussion.
2. Ask each student to write down three or four English insults.
3. Divide the class into groups of no more than four students.
4. Give each group a piece of poster board. Give each member of the group a different colored marker. Have the group members write their names at the bottom of the poster board in their own colors. (Using different colors encourages each person to contribute.) Let the groups choose group names and write them at the top of the poster board.
5. Ask each group to write eight insults on their poster board. Then have some or all of the groups hold up their posters and tell the class what the words mean and where they heard them.
6. As a class, discuss kind words—what they are, why people use them, and how they make others feel.
7. Ask each student to write down three or four kind words.
8. Distribute construction paper. Ask the students to draw two or three outlines of their feet, cut them out, and write one kind word on each foot.
9. Announce that your class is now going to "stamp out insults." Have the students glue or tape their paper feet over the insults listed on their poster board.
10. Give the groups a chance to tell about their posters. Display them in the classroom.

Caveats and Options

1. This lesson can be part of a focus on the social skill of being nice to others. Such a focus is especially appropriate in a class in which group activities are used. You can encourage students to continue using these kind words in their groups as well as at other times, both inside and outside of class.
2. This activity is a revised version of an idea from an elementary school teacher from Maui, Hawaii, who attended a course I taught on cooperative learning.

Contributor

George Jacobs teaches at the SEAMEO Regional Language Center, Singapore, Republic of Singapore.

My Name's Joshua, and I Like Dancing

Levels
Beginning

Aims
Practice introductions
Practice using *like* +
gerund

Class Time
10 minutes

Resources
A soft ball

Procedure

1. Ask the children to stand in a circle.
2. Give a soft ball to one of the children. Ask the child to throw the ball to someone else in the circle.
3. Have the person who catches the ball introduce himself or herself by saying, "My name's _____, and I like _____," miming an activity (e.g., dancing, singing, painting, playing the piano, eating, or swimming) without telling what it is. Tell the other children to guess what this child likes to do.
4. After everyone has had a turn, break up the circle and have the children move around the room freely, approaching other children and saying, "Your name's [Joshua], and you like [dancing]." Each correct statement is worth 1 point. When you stop the activity, the student with the most points is the winner.

Caveats and Options

1. Write a list of gerunds on the board to act as prompts for the children. Rub them off once the game is under way.
2. If the children in the class know each other very well, have them give themselves different names (e.g., the names of fairy-tale characters or film stars).

Contributor

Dino Mahoney teaches at the City University of Hong Kong.

Mix and Match

Levels
Beginning–intermediate

Aims
Develop vocabulary, both substantive and generic
Practice pronunciation
Develop abstract thinking about similarities and differences

Class Time
10 minutes

Resources
Open play area

Procedure

1. Divide the group into pairs.
2. Have each pair decide to be a set or a pair of something (e.g., salt and pepper, bacon and eggs, sweet and sour, cats and dogs). Each child is one thing or element in the pair or set.
3. Allow the players to scatter around the play area. Ask all players to close their eyes or put on blindfolds.
4. Have the players shout the name of the object in the pair that the other partner picked. The point of the game is to reunite the partners. The pandemonium of the search adds to the fun.
5. End the game when all pairs have been matched. The players open their eyes, and it is quiet.

Caveats and Options

1. A simple enhancement is to work with trios instead of pairs. Have the children identify one of the partners as the word that describes both elements in the pair. (For example, *condiments* goes with *salt* and *pepper, animals* with *cats* and *dogs*.) The object of the game is to reunite the trios.
2. If you need a more subdued version, have the participants write their identities on index cards. Writers can help emerging literate participants. Shuffle the cards and hand them out. Have the participants attempt to complete their pairs or trios by asking, "Are you a condiment?" or announcing to the group, "I'm looking for pepper." If most of the group doesn't read yet, set a rule of playing with whispers.
3. Play with opposites.

Contributors

Amy Schlessman and T. Frank Saunders are co-owners of Double Think, Inc., Tucson, Arizona, in the United States.

Origami Icebreaker

Levels
Beginning +

Aims
Practice counting
Practice spelling color
words
Ask *wh-* questions and
yes/no questions
Start a conversation
with people outside the
ESL classroom

Class Time
1 hour

Resources
Square pieces of paper
(approximately 8.5 in.
by 8.5 in.)
Pencils
Crayons or markers

Procedure

1. Give each child a square piece of paper.
2. Lead the children through the folding process:

   - Fold the paper into an even triangle.
   - Open the square and fold the paper into a triangle the other way.
   - Open the paper again. You should have four equal triangles.
   - Fold each corner into the center.
   - Turn the paper over and fold each corner into the center.
   - Fold and crease the square into a rectangle. Open it, and fold and crease it into a rectangle the other way. Open it again.

3. Show the students how to decorate their "icebreakers":

   - Turn the side with the four equal squares face up. Write the name of a color in each of the eight triangles. Then color the triangles.

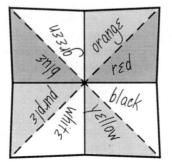

● Turn the icebreaker over and write a number between 1 and 20 in each of the eight triangles.

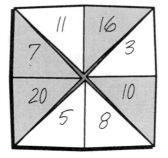

● Open the four flaps and write a question in each of the eight triangles (e.g., *What's your name? Where do you live? How old are you? What's the capital of Montana? Do you like ice cream? What's your favorite color? Do you speak Korean? What's your favorite sport?*)

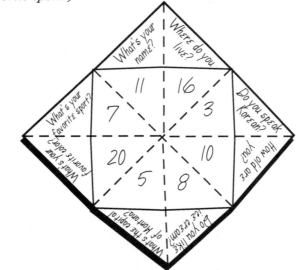

4. Show the students how to bring their origami icebreakers alive by placing their thumbs in the front pockets and two fingers of each hand in the back pockets. By opening and closing and pulling in the other direction, the students can make their icebreakers look like mouths opening and closing.
5. Demonstrate the following conversation:
   A: Pick a color [showing the top of the icebreaker].
   B: Blue.
   A: B-L-U-E [opening and closing the icebreaker in opposite directions for each letter]. Pick a number between 1 and 10.
   B: 5.
   A: 1, 2, 3, 4, 5 [opening and closing the icebreaker]. Pick another number [showing the eight numbers].
   B: 10.
   A: [opening the triangle marked 10] What's your favorite color?
   B: Green!
6. Have the students practice this conversation with at least five people outside the classroom (including at least two non-ESL students).

Caveats and Options

1. To practice the future tense, replace the questions with fortunes (e.g., *You will become president someday.*).
2. The icebreaker can be turned upside down and used as a candy dish.

Contributor

Christine Wagner-Jonsson teaches at Irving Elementary School, Bozeman, Montana, in the United States.

Preparing Young L2 Learners for the Inclusion of Children With Special Needs

Levels
Intermediate +

Aims
Develop the ethic of
caring for others
Engage in positive social
experiences in assisting
and learning from
children who are
differently abled

Class Time
35–60 minutes

Resources
Special-needs children
and special education
teacher
Time for the special edu-
cation and ESOL teachers
to plan for joint activity
*Russell Is Extra Special:
A Book about Autism for
Children* (Ameta, 1992)
Leo the Late Bloomer
(Aruego, 1971)
Additional materials for
joint activity as deter-
mined by special educa-
tion and ESOL teachers

Procedure

1. Read *Russell Is Extra Special: A Book about Autism for Children* (Ameta, 1992) to the ESOL children. Discuss the following questions:
   - What does it mean to be autistic?
   - How is Russell different from other children?
   - How is Russell similar to other children?
2. Prepare for the joint activity by discussing the following questions:
   - Where are we going?
   - What are we going to do?
   - What can we expect?
   - How can we help?
3. Do the joint activity with the special-needs children and special education teacher. Sample activities include doing an art project, making or eating lunch, playing on the playground, listening to a story, and singing a song in a circle.
4. Debrief by making a chart together of the new things the students learned by working together.
5. As a follow-up activity for ESOL students, read *Leo the Late Bloomer* (Aruego, 1971). Discuss Leo's feelings. Illustrate what Leo couldn't do before and what he could do after he "bloomed." Discuss why it is important for Leo's father to be patient and let Leo bloom.

Caveats and Options

1. A trend in school district restructuring in the U.S. is to implement new programs of inclusion of special education students in regular classrooms. Inclusion is different from mainstreaming. Examples of inclusion are children from an autistic kindergarten class having lunch with a regular second-grade class and participating in a music assembly with a group of classes. In elementary education, it is important that ESOL teachers and their students be a part of restructuring efforts to ensure that all children are included within the vision and mission of the school community.

2. The book on autism is an example of a children's book for only one special education population. The special education teacher will be able to assist you in identifying books that address other special populations in your school.

3. Beginning ESOL students can also work with special-needs children in mutually beneficial ways. For example, instead of reading *Russell Is Extra Special* (Ameta, 1992), look at the pictures with the children. Identify ways to use the L1 to increase understanding of autism and show beginning ESOL students how to help a special-needs child.

References and Further Reading

Ameta, C. A., III, M. D. (1992). *Russell is extra special: A book about autism for children*. New York: Magination Press.

Aruego, J. (1971). *Leo the late bloomer.* New York: Simon & Schuster.

Contributor

Shelley D. Wong teaches at the University of Maryland, College Park, Maryland, in the United States.

Part II: Real-Life Situations

Menus

Levels
Beginning–low
intermediate

Aims
Practice the
pronunciation of food
vocabulary
Practice spelling food
vocabulary
Reinforce the use of
money (counting and
making change)

Class Time
1 hour

Resources
Large pieces of
construction paper
Markers
Pens or pencils
Small pads of paper
Sample menus
Play money

Procedure

1. Show the students the sample menus, pointing out how foods and prices are listed.
2. Brainstorm categories of foods and the kinds of foods the students would like to eat.
3. Tell the students they will get to make their own menus with foods of their choice. Discuss prices.
4. Give each student a large piece of construction paper.
5. Show the students how to fold their paper in half and use it to make a menu, listing the foods and prices on the inside.

6. Let the students decorate the covers of their menus.
7. Use the menus to simulate ordering food in a restaurant: Have the students take turns being the customers and the waiters/waitresses. The students can write down the orders on a pad of paper, add up the bill, and use play money to pay for the food and receive change.

Caveats and Options

1. Discuss sales tax and tipping with advanced students.
2. Let the students cut out pictures of foods from magazines and supermarket advertisements and use the pictures to decorate their menus.
3. Have the students take "carry-out" orders from school personnel (e.g., office secretaries, principal) to provide practice speaking with other English speakers.

Contributor

Joan Dungey is an educational consultant in Yellow Springs, Ohio, in the United States.

Shopping for Furniture for a House

Levels
Beginning-low
intermediate

Aims
Practice pronouncing
and reading furniture
vocabulary
Reinforce money skills
(counting, making
change) and
measurement skills

Class Time
3 hours (for three
activities)

Resources
Poster board for each
student
Markers
Yardsticks
Glue or paste
Scissors
Catalogs and magazines
Newspaper
advertisements
Sample floor plan of a
house
Play money

Procedure

Introductory Activity

1. Show the students the sample floor plan of the house. Explain that it shows the house from above, looking down (without the roof on).
2. Draw a floor plan of your classroom together on poster board or on the chalkboard.
3. Extension: Lead the students to draw a floor plan of the school.

Activity I: "Building" a House

1. Give the students poster board and ask them to draw a floor plan of a house they would like to build. Help them measure with yardsticks and draw lines with markers.
2. Have the students label the rooms in their houses. Have older students mark doorways and halls.

Activity II: Making a Furniture Store

1. Give the students magazines, catalogs, and scissors. Let them select and cut out household items to sell in their own furniture stores. Tell them to include the price of each item.
2. Ask each student to select an area of the classroom to be his or her store, displaying the furniture for sale on a poster board, table, or desktop.

Activity III: Buying Furniture for a House

1. Give the students equal amounts of play money. Then let them go to their classmates' stores to buy furniture for their houses. Remind them that the furniture must fit inside the rooms.
2. Have the students practice buying and selling furniture, receiving money, and giving change.
3. Have the students paste the furniture they buy into the rooms of their houses.

Caveats and Options

1. You may wish to pair or group the students for these activities. The members of each small group can work together to build one house, make one furniture store, and buy furniture for their house.
2. If students don't see any furniture they like in their classmates' stores, let the shopkeepers search through catalogs and order the desired furniture for later delivery. Show the students how to give receipts.
3. If students buy furniture that does not fit into their houses, show them how to return it for a refund.

Contributor

Joan Dungey is an educational consultant in Yellow Springs, Ohio, in the United States.

Around Town

Levels
Beginning–intermediate

Aims
Practice vocabulary for buildings in a town
Practice verb tenses
Practice question word order

Class Time
Variable

Resources
6-in. by 18-in. white construction paper (one piece for each student)
Crayons

Caveats and Options

Contributor

Procedure

1. Ask the students to fold their piece of paper in half, then in half again the same way. Then have them open the paper and tape the ends together to form a four-sided building.
2. Have the students choose a building to illustrate (e.g., bank, drugstore, grocery store), and ask them to decorate both the outside (e.g., entrance, fire exits) and the inside (e.g., shelves, counter, cash register).
3. Set the buildings up as a Main Street and have the students take turns visiting the buildings (outside and inside) with a toy figure or toy car.
4. Model a sentence, such as "I went to the drugstore yesterday." Have the students respond, "What did you do there?" Reply, "I bought some bandages." Have the students ask, "Where did you go next?"
5. Allow each student to take a turn as the rest of the group asks questions.

Shift to the future tense using *going to* or *will*. For example, say, "I am going to go to the drugstore." Have the students respond, "What are you going to do there?" Answer, "I am going to buy some bandages." Have the students ask, "Where are you going to go next?"

Edith Fotopoulos teaches at Memorial School and Stony Lane School, Paramus, New Jersey, in the United States.

19

Classroom Store

Levels
Any

Aims
Build conversational skills in a simulated real-life situation
Reinforce vocabulary in a specific area of study
Reinforce math skills (counting money, figuring change)

Class Time
15–30 minutes

Resources
Play money
Items related to a category (e.g., food, school supplies, clothing)
Price list or signs

Procedure

1. Set up a store on a table or desktop. Arrange the items and price them.
2. Pass out equal amounts of play money to the children.
3. Have the children take turns visiting the store to request items, pay for them, and count their change.
4. Continue until all the money is spent.
5. Discuss the purchases of each customer, comparing what each one bought with the same amount of money.

Caveats and Options

1. Have the students take turns managing the store and making change.
2. Reinforce good manners and courtesy.
3. This activity is well suited to holiday times. For example, instead of having a Valentine's Day party, put Valentine treats such as stickers, candy, small cards, or cups of juice in the store for the children to purchase.

Contributor

Doris P. Mann teaches at Minor Elementary School, Lilburn, Georgia, in the United States.

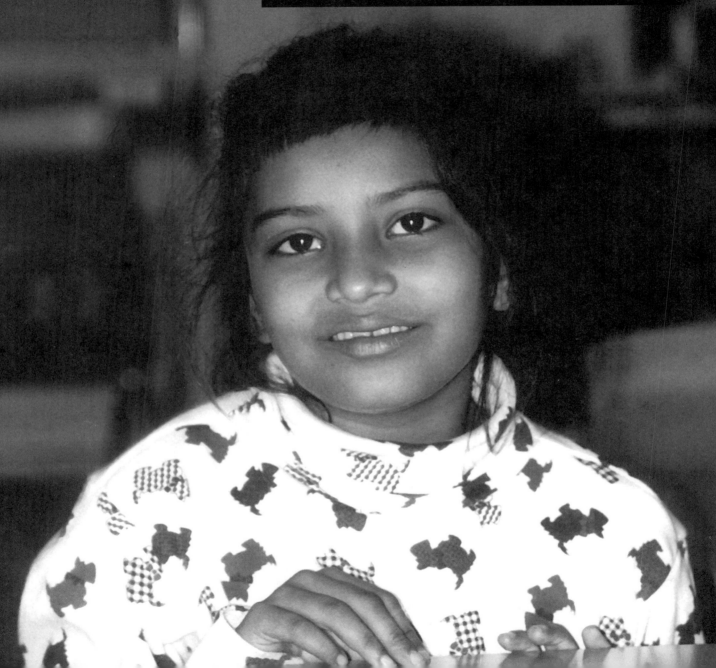

Part III: The Senses

Mandip Kaur at Kings Park Elementary School, Burke, Virginia, USA.

The Nose Knows

Levels
Beginning

Aims
Learn the names of
colors and common
foods
Use the sense of smell
to increase the retention
of information

Class Time
20 minutes

Resources
Set of scented markers
for each group of three
or four students
Blindfold for each group
of three or four students
Plastic food or pictures
of food
Cards showing the basic
colors

Procedure

1. Introduce the color words by using visual clues. Reinforce the color names by having the students tell their favorite colors. Discuss what each color makes the students think of. Relate the colors to items in nature (e.g., brown can be associated with mud, white with snow, red with flowers, and black with night).
2. Use visual clues to introduce the food items represented in your set of markers.
3. Divide the class into groups of three or four.
4. Tell the children in each group to take turns being blindfolded.
5. Have each blindfolded child smell a marker and try to guess the fruit (or other food) and the color of the marker. The goal is to have the children say a color word with only smell as a stimulus.
6. Review the color words using visual clues.
7. Review the food words using visual clues.
8. Evaluate mastery orally.

Caveats and Options

1. Expand the lesson by having the students draw pictures of all the foods they know that are yellow, green, red, and so on.
2. Use "scratch-and-sniff" stickers to teach additional food words. Follow the same procedure as for the markers.
3. Use this exercise as a springboard for a creative writing assignment that explores word associations. Have the class as a whole write a poem and illustrate it.

Contributor

Judith Cloutier teaches at Roosevelt Roads Elementary School, Roosevelt Roads Naval Station, in Puerto Rico.

Smell-a-Vision

Levels
Beginning

Aims
Learn new vocabulary
and/or review
vocabulary
Use the sense of smell
to reinforce learning

Class Time
10 minutes

Resources
One blindfold
Four or five items with
strong aromas (e.g.,
perfume, coffee,
cinnamon, cheese)

Procedure

1. Introduce or review the names of the aromatic items.
2. Invite one student to the front of the room and blindfold him or her.
3. Put one of the aromatic items in front of the student's nose.
4. Let the student guess what the item is. Remove the blindfold.
5. Repeat with the other students.

Caveats and Options

1. This activity may be useful as a summary and review for a unit on food.
2. This format can also be used for tasting foods and feeling and identifying objects.

Contributor

Leslie Cohen teaches in Kibbutz Ein Hashofet, Israel.

Silent Words

Procedure

1. Review the vocabulary or pronunciation items you wish to practice.
2. Mouth one of the words, sentences, or other items without saying it aloud. Let the children read your lips and try to figure out what you're saying. Have them guess aloud.
3. After someone has guessed correctly, have the entire class repeat the word or sentence.
4. Repeat with the other items on your list.

Caveats and Options

1. As a recall exercise at the end of the activity, ask the children how many of the items they remember.
2. Conduct the activity as a group or pair activity.

Sally Galili teaches in Kibbutz Ein Hamifratz, Israel.

Contributor

Telepathy Vocabulary

Levels
Beginning +

Aims
Practice reading and/or
pronouncing previously
learned vocabulary

Class Time
5 minutes

Resources
Cards with words or
pictures (one word or
picture per card)

Contributor

Procedure

1. Review the vocabulary you wish to practice, showing the cards as you do so.
2. Shuffle the cards.
3. Hold up one card so that the students cannot see the word or picture on it. Tell the children to "feel" or guess what the word or picture is. If a child guesses correctly, give the card to that child.
4. Repeat with the rest of the cards.

Caveats and Options

This can be organized as a group activity.

Sally Galili teaches in Kibbutz Ein Hamifratz, Israel.

Whisper Circles

Levels
Beginning–intermediate

Aims
Practice pronunciation
and articulation of
words and short phrases

Class Time
10 minutes

Resources
Card containing a short
sentence or phrase

Procedure

1. Seat the children in a circle.
2. Give one of the more linguistically proficient children a card with a short phrase on it (e.g., *The cow jumped over the moon.*). Ask the child to memorize the phrase.
3. Take the card away from the child and ask her or him to whisper what was written on the card to the child on the right. The child can repeat the whispered phrase only once.
4. Have that child whisper the phrase to the next child on the right, and so on around the circle.
5. Ask the last child to hear the phrase to say it out loud. Then ask the child who started the whisper circle to read aloud what was written on the card. Often the final phrase is not the phrase written on the card. For example, *The cow jumped over the moon* might become *The cat jumped over a spoon.* The children may find this very amusing and spontaneously start to explore, in the target language, how the phrase changed.

Caveats and Options

1. Begin the whisper circle with one word only before building up to a phrase.
2. If your class is quite large, seat the children in more than one circle and give a different card to each group for its whisper circle.
3. Use tongue twisters, such as *red leather, yellow leather.*
4. Use whisper circles to practice words containing sounds that are difficult for your students (e.g., *the red lion roared* for Cantonese- and Mandarin-speaking children).

Contributor

Dino Mahoney teaches at the City University of Hong Kong.

Make It Real

Levels
Beginning +

Aims
Develop and expand
Vocabulary Word Banks
through brainstorming
Participate in a shared
experience to stimulate
writing

Class Time
30–45 minutes
(depending on the
amount of time devoted
to oral sharing)

Resources
8-in. by 10-in. paper,
one piece for each
student
Tantalizing food item
(enough for the entire
class), such as chocolate
cake with vanilla
frosting or apple pie

Procedure

1. Have the students fold the paper into four sections and unfold it. The four resulting sections will be used to record four separate Vocabulary Word Banks based on sensory reactions to and perceptions of the food item, in this case chocolate cake.
2. Have the students label each of the sections with one of the following headings:
   - How does it make me feel?
   - How does it smell?
   - How does it taste?
   - How does it feel?
3. Hold up the cake. Allow the children to look at it and examine it for the first time. Ask them to think of as many words or phrases as possible to describe how they felt when they saw the cake.
4. After 1 minute of silent reflection time (SRT), have the students write their responses under the heading *How does it make me feel?*
5. Now give each child a piece of cake. Invite the children to enjoy its aroma. Ask, "What does it remind you of? What does it smell like?" Repeat SRT. Ask the students to list words or phrases under the corresponding heading.
6. Finally, taste the cake. Ask the children for words that describe the taste of the cake and frosting. Ask, "What does it taste like?" Have the students write words or phrases under the corresponding heading.
7. Ask, "How does it feel in your mouth, on your tongue, as you chew it, when you swallow it?" List words and phrases to describe these feelings in the remaining section.

Caveats and Options

1. The use of food usually achieves a guaranteed reaction. The reaction may be negative or positive, but either way it is a stimulus for writing.
2. Have the students work individually, in pairs, or in small groups. If they are working with partners or cooperative groups, have them share their reflections orally at each step before they write. Have the students begin in one mode and shift to another in order to stretch interaction and to encourage diverse responses, idea generation, and opinions. If they are working in cooperative groups, give one piece of paper to each group and assign a scribe to record group members' responses.
3. Have the students share their Word Banks with a partner or with small groups.
4. Ask the students to use the Word Banks to write a poem or story. Be sure to include metaphors, similes, and adjectives to make the cake come to life. Throughout the writing process, have the students share their work and receive feedback from their classmates through the process of peer revision and teacher/student conferences.
5. Display the Word Banks on chart paper around the classroom for use in subsequent lessons.
6. Integrate this lesson with science lessons such as a study of the five senses and with math lessons such as measuring ingredients and cooking.
7. Have the students make a class book related to food or to the five senses, with each student contributing a page with text and drawings. Laminate the book and make it available for students to take home to read to their families.

Contributor

Grace Indoccio Matty is an educational resource specialist at the Urban Teacher Resource Center, Lowell, Massachusetts, in the United States.

Walking Trips

Levels
Levels
Beginning–low intermediate

Aims
Aims
Develop perceptual skills related to sight, smell, touch, taste, and sound
Compare and contrast objects, events, and/or experiences
Label and classify things observed
Predict possible causes and effects

Class Time
Class Time
Entire class period for each walk

Resources
Resources
Areas for exploration (school buildings and grounds, a neighborhood)
Pictures of people displaying various feelings
Art supplies
Small containers (Puddle Walk)
Camera (Windy Day Walk)
Electric fan (Windy Day Walk)

Procedure

1. Initiate or have the students initiate a focus and goal before each walking trip. This may be done by talking about a special thing seen on the way to school, sharing a discovery made in the neighborhood, discussing some questions raised by an observed phenomenon, inviting a resource person to explain his or her role in the neighborhood, expanding on a building project started in the block center, or noting some interesting conditions in the neighborhood.

2. Discuss expectations for the trip and how best to accomplish them. Share decision making, such as which ways would be appropriate to collect and record information sought (e.g., cameras, tape recorders, sketch pads); the most efficient grouping of efforts (small groups or individuals); safety precautions and procedures; which materials and equipment to take on the trip (e.g., first-aid kit, compass); and the responsibility for getting all permissions and clearances necessary for the trip.

3. On the walk, have accompanying adults provide focus or provoke attention with the types of questions they ask the students. Examples of such questions are *What makes puddles different in size and shape? Why would a bug make a home under a rock? What kinds of things can you learn about an insect by watching it?*

4. For a Feeling Walk:
   - Before the walk, read *The Ugly Duckling* by Hans Christian Andersen to the children and discuss and develop a Feeling Chart for the duckling's many feelings throughout the story.
   - Have the children take a walk through the school halls and on the playground to observe and record facial expressions that reveal feelings.

30

- Have the children discuss and share their recorded words and sketches made on the trip.
- Use pictures, photos, and sketches that depict all kinds of feelings. Have the children list alternative adjectives that describe the feeling.
- Provide a variety of art media so that each child may try different media and colors to express feelings.
- Using feeling words (e.g., *angry, startled, happy, gloomy, giggly*), have the children demonstrate how they would walk, or have them use nonverbal communication to convey the various feelings.
- Ask the children to write a fantasy story about a Feeling picture, or have them write in their journals concerning their own feelings.

Caveats and Options

1. For a Puddle Walk:
    - Have the children walk around the school neighborhood after a rain. Take containers for samples and note the color, size, depth, and location of puddles.
    - After the walk, discuss and record some of the children's observations about puddles. Talk about how the samples could be used.
    - Have the children draw maps that show the location of each puddle explored.
    - Alter the song "Old MacDonald Had a Farm" to "Old MacDonald Has a Puddle." Use words from observations on the walk in the song.
2. For a Windy Day Walk:
    - Before the walk, turn a revolving fan on and discuss the effects of it. List the responses on a chart.
    - Walk around the schoolyard on a windy day. Have the children observe how the wind is affecting birds, animals, plants, soil, and people. Take along notepads and a camera, if possible.
    - After the walk, discuss and compare the children's observations about the wind and its effects to the chart of wind words. Add adjectives and verbs to the wind chart.

- Read "The Wind" by Robert L. Stevenson. Compare the words he used to illustrate the wind's moving action with the children's words.
- Let the children express wind movements with scarves and music, or have them act out the poem "Wind Capers" by Nancy Byrd Turner.
- Have the children look at a number of weather reports from newspapers and almanacs.
- Ask the children to write a real or fantasy story about the wind, write in their journals about their wind walk experience, or write a poem about the wind.

References and Further Reading

The booklet *26 Ways to Walk* by Bette Dehls is available from TEEM Follow Through, University of Arizona, College of Education, Tucson, Arizona 58721 U.S.A.

Contributors

Alice Paul and Amy Schlessman were educational specialists with the Tucson Early Education Model at the University of Arizona, Tucson, in the United States.

Part IV: Learning Through Actions

Left to right: Chan-Hyuk Kang, Michael Stirling, and Su Han Kim at Kings Park Elementary School, Burke, Virginia, USA.

The Superlative Adjective Adventure

Levels
Beginning–intermediate

Aims
Develop communicative
ability in both speaking
and listening
Practice reading and
writing skills
Review vocabulary for
parts of the body
Review superlative
adjectives
Practice using
mathematical concepts

Class Time
1–1½ hours

Resources
Chalkboard or overhead
projector
Meter sticks or
yardsticks
12-in. or 30-cm rulers
Paper
Pens or pencils

Procedure

1. Introduce the topic of superlative adjectives by writing the words *Adjective Adventure* on the board. Then give an example, such as *longest hair*.
2. Brainstorm other examples for the adventure, such as *widest palms*, *smallest feet*, *funniest person*, and *tallest person*. Write 10 examples on the board. Be careful to avoid potentially offensive or embarrassing examples such as *fattest*, *thinnest*, *smartest*, and so on.
3. Divide the class into groups of four or five. Give each group a ruler and a meter stick or yardstick.
4. Have the groups determine which member represents each category and write their findings (e.g., *Lucia has the smallest feet*).
5. Let the groups compare their results.
6. Ask a "reporter" to give the figures for each group. From the information displayed on the board, have the students compile written reports about the facts they learned while on their Adjective Adventure.

Caveats and Options

Have students who are not yet readers or writers in the L2 draw pictures as you introduce each concept to help them understand the vocabulary used in this exercise.

Contributor

Sean Bracken teaches in Port Vila, Vanatu, in the South Pacific.

Listening Comprehension Through Pictures

Levels
Beginning

Aims
Demonstrate vocabulary
comprehension by
performing required
actions

Class Time
15 minutes

Resources
Reproducible picture
(perhaps one that
represents a holiday or
special occasion)
Crayons or markers
List of target vocabulary
(including objects in the
picture and words used
for directions, such as
colors or prepositions)

Procedure

1. Give each child a copy of the picture and some crayons or markers.
2. Give directions using the target vocabulary. (For example, if your target vocabulary includes colors, say, "Color the dog black. Color the house red. Color the fence brown." If your target vocabulary includes prepositions, say, "Draw a line under the dog. Draw a line over the house. Draw a circle around the tree. Draw an *X* on the fence.")

Caveats and Options

Pair the children or group them cooperatively for this activity and allow them to give each other directions.

Contributor

Judi Braverman teaches at the Lindell School, Long Beach, New York, in the United States.

Jumping on Colors

Levels
Beginning

Aims
Practice recognizing
color names
Demonstrate listening
comprehension through
actions

Class Time
10-15 minutes

Resources
Pieces of colored paper

Procedure

1. Lay pieces of colored paper (four or five sheets of each color) on the floor. Leave some space between the papers.
2. Ask the children to take off their shoes.
3. Call out a color. Have the students find that color and stand on it.
4. Once all the squares of that color are occupied by students, call out a new color.

Caveats and Options

1. There are no winners or losers in this game. The goal is to practice recognizing as many color names as possible.
2. Practice *left* and *right* by calling out "left foot" or "right foot" with the color names (e.g., "Left foot green, right foot pink").
3. To practice shapes as well as colors, use plain white paper with one colored shape on each piece (e.g., a red circle, a blue triangle, a yellow square). Make sure you have several sheets with each combination. Call out directions such as "red circle" and "blue triangle."
4. Instead of calling out the directions yourself, write them on cards and let the students take turns calling them out (from words or small illustrations).
5. Do this activity with pictures representing vocabulary groups such as animals, numbers, and family members. It is an enjoyable way to practice listening while allowing the children to use some of their energy.
6. If you are using colored shapes glued on white paper, have the students make these as a pregame activity. The sheets used in this game are hardly ever reusable.

Contributor

Keith Folse is the author of several books for The University of Michigan Press.

Individual White Boards

Levels
Any

Aims
Practice following
directions
Review vocabulary
Use spontaneity and
inquisitiveness

Class Time
20 minutes

Resources
White boards (one per
student or team)
Colored white board
markers
Picture cards (optional)
Small colored magnets
(optional)

Procedure

1. Give each student a white board and a marker. (If you have a large class, make teams and give each team a white board and a marker.)
2. Give a command, such as "Draw a cat" or "Write the word *cat*."
3. Have the students listen and follow your command. Award points for correct answers.
4. Give new instructions, changing the item to be drawn, until the students have mastered the command (e.g., "Draw one red apple.").
5. At the end of the activity, declare the student or team with the most points the winner.

Caveats and Options

1. For a more collaborative learning activity, have the students sit in groups of three or four, but give each student a white board and a marker. Let the group members compare their answers after they finish drawing.
2. Prepare cards with pictures of familiar objects. Choose a student to become the "teacher." The "teacher" selects a card without showing it to anyone and then tells the other students what to draw.
3. Use the colored magnets to demonstrate parts of speech, such as prepositions. For example, let a blue magnet represent a chair and a red magnet a table. Give instructions such as "Put the table next to the chair" or "Put the chair under the table."

4. Using white boards adds an element of fun to lessons and helps to fix visual as well as verbal images in the students' brains. The possibilities for their use are limitless: *yes/no* games, spelling games, counting games with magnets, and so on. Adults enjoy using white boards as much as children do.

Contributor

Diane Huntoon teaches at the Language Academy, Maebashi, Gunma, Japan.

Hop, Skip, and Jump a Word

Levels
Beginning

Aims
Practice listening to
letters or words
Practice spelling words
Practice action verbs

Class Time
10–15 minutes

Resources
Large alphabet cards on
thick paper

Procedure

1. Scatter the alphabet cards on the floor, leaving small spaces between the cards.
2. Have the children form a line near the cards.
3. If the children are real beginners, say a verb and a letter of the alphabet, such as "Jump. B." Have the first child in line jump onto B.
4. Then say another verb and letter of the alphabet, such as "Hop. G." Have the child hop onto G.
5. Continue until the child has moved to several letters using a different action each time. Once the child has finished his or her letters and actions, the child should move to the back of the line and allow the next child to begin. Keep the pace brisk.

Caveats and Options

1. Instead of saying the name of each letter, sound it out phonetically.
2. If the children are more advanced, say an action and a word, such as "Jump. Dark." Have the first child jump to the letters that spell the word in sequence. Ask the child to say each letter as he or she lands on it. Continue until each child has spelled five words.
3. Have the children themselves say the letters or words in a team challenge. For example, Team A can say words or letters for Team B and vice versa. The teacher becomes a facilitator by helping when there is a mistake and by keeping score on the board. Doing the activity this way increases student investment and motivation.

Contributor

Lesley Koustaff is ELT acquisitions editor for Prentice Hall Regents (Japan) in Tokyo, Japan.

Swat!

Levels
Beginning

Aims
Increase receptive
vocabulary
Demonstrate listening
comprehension
Practice speech
production

Class Time
10–15 minutes

Resources
Sets of related pictures
mounted on heavy
paper or cardboard
Different-colored
flyswatters (one for
every two children)

Contributor

Procedure

1. Lay the pictures on the floor and seat the children in a circle around them. Give every other child a flyswatter.
2. Give a command to swat one of the pictures (e.g., "Swat the dog.").
3. Have the children holding flyswatters attempt to follow your command.
4. If necessary, announce which swatters were successful (e.g., "Red [color of flyswatter] found it.").
5. Have the children pass the flyswatters to the right. Continue with another command.
6. After several rounds, replace the pictures with new ones.

Caveats and Options

1. Once the children know the names of all the items in a set of pictures (such as animals or foods), call out brief descriptions of the items (e.g., "It is black and white.").
2. Let the children take turns being the caller, initially using single words and later using short descriptions.

Victoria Marone teaches in the Milwaukee Public Schools, Milwaukee, Wisconsin, in the United States.

Self-Access Study Session

Levels
Intermediate +

Aims
Develop autonomy
Practice recently learned
material

Class Time
Entire class period

Resources
Activity centers in room
Question-and-answer
sheets for each center
Feedback forms

Caveats and Options

Procedure

1. Prepare different activities in advance and arrange them around the room. The activities used may be games, worksheets, readers, a listening corner (a tape recorder, earphones, and a choice of cassettes), and any other tasks that students can do on their own.

2. When the students come in, instruct them to pick an activity and spend the whole lesson working, moving to a different task if and when they choose.

3. Move around the room, observing and monitoring the children and helping when required.

4. At the end of the lesson, have the students fill in a feedback form. (This can be done in the L1.) On this form, ask the students to write the names of the activities they used, why they chose them, whether or not they enjoyed them, and whether or not they learned from them.

1. This lesson format makes it possible for the teacher to pay more attention to students who need help while the other students work by themselves.

2. This type of lesson may provide a welcome break in the regular lesson pattern for both students and teacher as well as being popular with the students.

3. Have the students spend the whole lesson working by themselves or with other students in small groups.

4. Provide enough activities for all the children, plus a few extra, so that every student, regardless of ability level, can find something to do. The activities should provide opportunities for group work, pair work, and individual work.

5. Other forms of feedback are also possible. For example, have the students do all the tasks in a notebook, which you can check regularly.

Contributor

Orly Sela teaches at Har-Vagai School, Kibbutz Dafna, Israel.

Part V: Realia

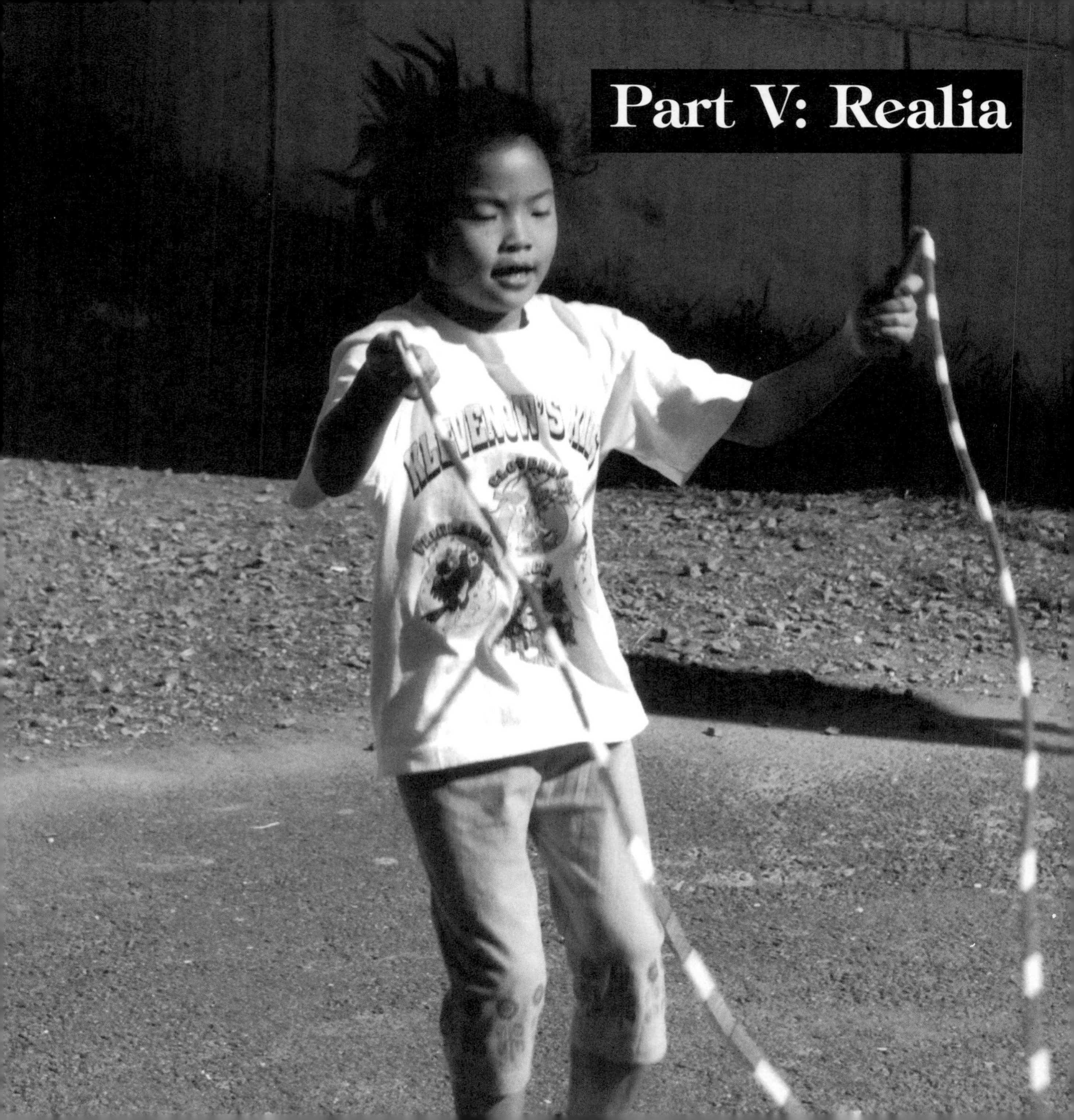

Meena Na at Kings Park Elementary School, Burke, Virginia, USA.

Name That Object

Levels
Beginning

Aims
Gain self-confidence in
speaking English
Practice vocabulary
related to a theme

Class Time
10–15 minutes

Resources
Paper bag or box
Objects related to a
topic or skills being
taught (e.g., fruits,
shapes, toys, colors)

Procedure

1. Seat the children in a circle. Give the bag or box of objects to the first child.
2. Tell the child to select one object from the bag and give its name both in English and in his or her native language.
3. If the child answers correctly, place the object in the middle of the circle. If not, replace the object in the bag.
4. Continue until all the objects are in the middle of the circle.

Caveats and Options

1. This activity is excellent for prereaders and beginning English speakers. It offers a nonthreatening way for children to build self-esteem and make concrete connections between English and their native language.
2. Reinforce the oral language further by having all the children repeat the words at the end of the exercise.
3. Use this game regularly and thematically (e.g., a week with fruits, the next with vegetables, the next with shapes) to help the children become very comfortable and familiar with it.
4. If you like, allow the children to help classmates who are having problems with a particular object.
5. This activity is also helpful for monolingual English speakers, as they will hear objects named in another language. It can help build self-esteem for both monolingual English speakers and non-English speakers in a bilingual classroom.

Contributors

María Artiaga and Lari Cobos teach at MacArthur Elementary School, Las Cruces, New Mexico, in the United States.

Mystery Box

Levels
Beginning

Aims
Practice the simple
question form *Is it
a _____?*
Review vocabulary (e.g.,
animal names)

Class Time
5–10 minutes

Resources
Small box that opens
easily (preferably from
the top)
Bag of toy animals (or
other items) that fit in
the box

Procedure

1. Before class, put one animal in the box.
2. Show the box to the class and say, "There is an animal in the box. What animal is it?"
3. Let the students take turns asking "Is it a _____?"
4. When a student guesses correctly, have him or her come to the front of the room, select another toy animal (from the closed bag), put it in the box, and call on other students to guess what is in the box.

Caveats and Options

1. To review the topic of clothing, bring a variety of clothing items and use a small suitcase instead of a box.
2. To review the topic of food, bring a variety of food items and use a grocery bag or basket instead of the box.

Leslie Cohen teaches in Kibbutz Ein Hashofet, Israel.

Contributor

House Decorators

Levels
Intermediate

Aims
Review vocabulary of
the house, rooms, and
furniture
Practice prepositions
and directions

Class Time
15–30 minutes

Resources
Several copies of a floor
plan of a house
Magazine pictures of
furniture and appliances
(four or five items for
each room in the floor
plan)
3-in. by 5-in. cards with
descriptions of each
room (including
directions for where to
put each item of
furniture in the room)

Procedure

1. Divide the class into groups of three. Give each group a copy of the floor plan and a card for a particular room in the house (e.g., the bedroom, the living room).
2. Place the pictures of furniture in a box. Have one member of each group come up and take three pictures from the box.
3. Tell the groups to read their cards and see what furniture they need and what they have. Explain that they must get the rest of the furniture they need from the other groups by making requests, such as "Do you have a bookshelf, please?" or "We need a dining room table."
4. When a group has all the pictures it needs, have the members place the furniture on the floor plan, following the description on their card.

Caveats and Options

The group members may compose a story about their house, describing the people who live in it. Let each group read its story to the class.

Contributor

Ronald Jackup is a freelance EFL teacher and writer.

Where Is It?

Levels
Beginning

Aims
Practice asking
questions
Practice using
prepositional phrases

Class Time
10–15 minutes

Resources
Stuffed animal or other
small toy

Contributor

Procedure

1. Show the class a stuffed animal or other small item.
2. Ask the students to close their eyes and count to 10 while you hide the item somewhere in the classroom.
3. Have the students ask questions to try to find out where the item is, such as *Is it in your desk?* or *Is it behind the picture?* The first child to guess where the item is gets to hide it again for the others to guess.

Caveats and Options

Ask the students questions to practice long or short answers, such as *Yes, the monkey is in my desk* and *Yes, it is./No, it isn't.*

Richard Jacobs is an independent EFL consultant.

Buttons, Buttons, Buttons

Levels
Beginning–intermediate

Aims
Develop critical
thinking skills through a
sorting and classifying
activity

Class Time
45 minutes

Resources
Buttons of different
shapes, sizes, colors,
and textures
Boxes, baskets, or
dishes to hold buttons
Chart paper

Contributor

Procedure

1. Sit in a circle with the children. Place the container of buttons in the middle. Take out some of the buttons one at a time, and have the children describe them. You can write the words on chart paper as the children think of them (e.g., *round*, *black*, *smooth*).
2. After you have discussed all the different qualities that the buttons have, ask the students to think of ways that the buttons can be grouped into piles that are the same. Try to elicit many different ways (e.g., by color, shape, texture; buttons with two holes, four holes).
3. Divide the class into small groups of three or four children each. Give each group a box or dish of buttons to sort and classify. Allow the children to sort the buttons any way they wish, or tell them which way you want them to sort.

Caveats and Options

Make a chart with each category (rough, square, etc.), and have the children think of other things that have those characteristics.

Esperanza Saludes Jacobson teaches at Hampton Street Elementary School, Mineola, New York, in the United States.

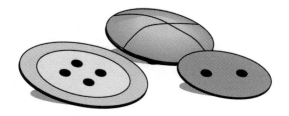

Label the Classroom

Levels
Beginning

Aims
Understand the names
of the main parts of and
objects in the classroom
environment (e.g., *door,
window, floor, light,
plant*)
Reinforce the names of
colors

Class Time
15–20 minutes

Resources
Sets of moderate-sized
cards, each card with
the name of a classroom
part or object and each
set written in a different
color (one set per team
of students)
Roll of adhesive tape

Procedure

1. Through listening and reading practice, familiarize the students with the names of the main classroom parts and objects to be learned.
2. Divide the class into several teams corresponding to the number of sets of cards prepared and let each team sit around a table or in a circle on the floor.
3. Give each team a set of cards.
4. Name each team after the color of its card set.
5. Let each team randomly display the cards face up.
6. Say one of the names to be identified.
7. Have whoever finds the relevant card in his or her team hold it up. (If the students cannot find the relevant card, give them a hint such as /d/ *desk*, pronouncing the initial sound of the word separately and emphatically followed by the full word.) Tell the students to keep holding up the card until they are told otherwise.
8. Decide which team is the fastest, and ask the student from that team who is holding up the card to point at the relevant item in the classroom.
9. If the student points at the correct item, award a point to that student's team. If the student gets it wrong, move on to the next fastest team, and so on.
10. When a team finds the correct item, let one student from each team walk to the object or part and stick the card on, near, or under it.
11. Continue the game until all the cards have been used.
12. At the end of the game, tally the score of each team with the help of the students. The team with the most points wins.

Caveats and Options

1. This Total Physical Response activity is particularly useful at the beginning of the semester for helping students to become familiar with their classroom environment.
2. If the class is very low level, focus on one team only for each card as a warm-up activity before doing the full-scale game.
3. Let each team choose a representative. Let the representatives compete with each other in taking down the labels each time you mention one. You can also let all team members participate in removing the labels.

Contributors

Elizabeth Lange teaches at Temple University Japan in Tokyo. Jong-Oe Park is a former EFL teacher in Korea and Japan.

Part VI: Literature

Comic Strip Sequencing

Levels
Low intermediate +

Aims
Practice reading
Practice sequencing
Write complete
sentences (for options)

Class Time
30 minutes

Resources
Comic sections from
newspapers
Scissors
Glue
Construction paper
Pencils or pens
Envelopes or paper clips

Procedure

1. Give each student the comic section of a newspaper (preferably from the Sunday section). Ask the students to select a comic strip they like.
2. Have the students paste the comic strip on a piece of construction paper and then cut the frames apart. Ask them to put the frames in an envelope or paper clip the frames together.
3. Let the students trade comic strips with a partner and try to put their partner's strip back into a logical order. Stress that it does not have to be in the original order as long as it makes sense.
4. Have the students check with their partner to see if they sequenced the comic strip correctly, or at least logically.

Caveats and Options

1. Ask the students to write at least one sentence for every frame of the comic strip. Number the sentences by frame.
2. For more advanced students, show how quotation marks are used. The students should then use proper punctuation for all dialogue that they write.
3. Cut out the dialogue balloons, and let the students try to make a story from them.

Contributor

Joan Dungey is an educational consultant in Yellow Springs, Ohio, in the United States.

Why We Have Winter

Levels
Intermediate

Aims
Gain background in
Western mythology
Develop writing skills

Class Time
Two 1-hour sessions

Resources
Copy of the story "Why
We Have Winter" for
each child (see
Appendix)
Props as desired for play
production

Procedure

1. Assign the story "Why We Have Winter" for homework.
2. Divide class into small groups to rewrite the story in play format. Use the following characters: Zeus, Hades, Demeter, Persephone, Iris, Helios, and Friends of Persephone.
3. Produce the play as written by the children.

Caveats and Options

The three sections of the story correspond to three acts of the play.

Appendix: Text of "Why We Have Winter"

Section 1

Long ago many people believed that gods and goddesses were in charge of all parts of the universe. Among these was Demeter, the goddess of the earth. She was in charge of the flowers, the trees, and the fruits of many plants. She made a beautiful world for human beings.

Demeter had a lovely daughter, and her name was Persephone. Persephone spent most of her time playing among the flowers with her friends. She was very beautiful and very kind, and everyone loved her dearly.

There was a powerful god named Hades (also known as Pluto), and he was king of the Underworld. That was a dark place where all the dead were kept. It was in the center of the earth, and no light ever entered there. Hades spent most of his time there, but on one trip to the Upperworld, he happened to see Persephone.

Persephone was running about in a field, gathering flowers with her friends, laughing and shouting. Her grace and beauty made Hades fall in love with her immediately, and he wanted her to be his wife. He knew that she would not want to leave the world of light and beauty, so he asked Zeus, the king of all the gods, to help him.

Zeus made a lovely, fragrant flower appear just beyond where Persephone was playing with her friends. As soon as she spotted the flower, she left her friends and ran over to pick it. Just as she put out her hand, the earth broke open, and a great black chariot with great black horses drove out. King Hades himself was driving, and he caught Persephone up with one arm and drove off with her, down to his dark world.

Section 2

Persephone cried out for help. Demeter heard her, but she could not find her daughter. She went around asking everyone if they had seen anything, but no one could help her. Finally, she asked Helios, the sun, who sees everything. He told her, "I will tell you, Demeter, Zeus did this. He made it possible for King Hades to kidnap Persephone, and she is now his wife, the queen of the Underworld."

Demeter was very unhappy without her daughter. In fact, she was so unhappy that she wanted everyone else to be unhappy, too. She used her power as goddess of the earth to cause a terrible time on the farms. Seeds did not sprout, and there were no harvests, fruits, or vegetables of any kind. Everywhere people were starving.

Section 3

Zeus saw what was happening, and he sent Iris, the messenger of the gods, to Demeter. Iris asked Demeter to come to a meeting, but Demeter was very angry with Zeus, so she refused to go.

Then Zeus sent a message to Hades that Persephone had to return to earth because her mother might destroy all mankind since there was no food. Hades was sad, but he knew he had to let Persephone return to her mother. However, before she left, he wanted her to eat something. Persephone was so happy to be going home that she swallowed seven pomegranate seeds quickly and got ready to go.

Then Hades got out his chariot and drove her back to Demeter. When she saw her mother, Persephone jumped out of the chariot and ran to her. They hugged and kissed.

Then Demeter asked, "Persephone, did you eat any food while you were in the Dark Kingdom? If you have eaten anything, you must return to the Underworld."

Of course, Hades had known this, and that was why he wanted her to eat something before she left his kingdom. However, Zeus was afraid that Demeter would destroy all the crops forever if she lost her daughter again, so he had to figure a way out.

He thought hard and finally decided that Persephone should spend part of the year with Hades and part of the year with her mother. In this way, both Demeter and Hades would have time with the beautiful girl.

So it is that when Persephone goes down to the Dark Kingdom, Demeter is lonely and unhappy, and she does not keep up with her goddess of the earth duties. It is wintertime on earth, and crops do not grow. People cannot work in the fields.

When Persephone returns in the springtime and Demeter is contented, she fills the world with green leaves, blooming flowers, and ripening grain. The whole earth is as happy as Persephone and Demeter.

Contributor

Mary Everett teaches at Kansai Gaidai University, Osaka, Japan.

Teaching Prepositions With Nursery Rhymes

Procedure

Levels
Beginning–low
intermediate

Aims
Learn prepositions using
nursery rhymes

Class Time
45 minutes per rhyme

Resources
Chart paper
Markers or crayons
Words to various
nursery rhymes
Felt board
Felt pieces with pictures
for each rhyme (can be
made by gluing picture
to oaktag and oaktag to
felt)

1. Introduce the children to nursery rhymes with a book that contains several different ones. Explain what they are, and after reading a few, try to elicit why they are called nursery rhymes. After this introduction, begin to go into further detail with one rhyme at a time (perhaps one each day).
2. Write the rhyme for the day on chart paper and attach a picture of it, or illustrate it yourself underneath the words.
3. Practice reading the rhyme together with the students, pointing to each word as you read. Point out where the words rhyme, and discuss the fact that some rhyming words look alike and others do not. (You can color code the rhyming words.)
4. Take the felt pieces and place them out of sequence on the flannel board. Have the children work together to figure out where the pieces should go.
5. Act out the rhyme with the felt characters and/or have the children act as the characters.
6. Once the children have internalized the nursery rhyme, have them come up to the flannel board one at a time and move the pieces around. Ask "Who can come up and put Humpty Dumpty under the wall?" or "Where would Humpty Dumpty be if he were to sit behind the wall?" If the children do not know some of the prepositions, model them first several times using the felt pieces. Have the children repeat each new "place" where you put Humpty. Then ask the children to come up and try to place the pieces on their own.
7. As a follow-up activity, give each child a copy of the words to illustrate. To check the students' comprehension, look to see that all or most of the elements of the rhyme are in their illustrations (e.g.,

Humpty Dumpty, a wall, horses, and men). Collect the illustrations and assemble them into a Nursery Rhyme Book for each child. As the children learn and illustrate each rhyme, they can add it to their books to take home at the end of the unit.

Caveats and Options

1. Depending on the level of the students, either teach several prepositions by concentrating on only one rhyme (e.g., "Humpty Dumpty," as explained above, or "Little Miss Muffet"—"Where did the spider sit?"), or work on one or two prepositions at a time and manipulate the rhymes to fit only those being taught.
2. Write the words on sentence strips, and have students practice putting the words to each sentence in the correct order. Then ask questions like "Which words tell where Humpty Dumpty is?" and other similar questions that can check the students' understanding of the material.
3. Practice using prepositions with a chair. Have the children (either one at a time or all together if there are enough chairs) perform the action of the preposition that you say. For example, say, "Tina, can you come up here and stand behind this chair?" or "Everyone should stand in front of his or her chair." If you ask the children one at a time, you can check their understanding better because they can no longer follow the other children. However, be aware that some children will not react well to being singled out, particularly those still in the silent period.

Contributor

Esperanza Saludes Jacobson teaches at Hampton Street Elementary School, Mineola, New York, in the United States.

Writing New Versions of Popular Children's Literature

Levels
Advanced beginning–
intermediate

Aims
Acquire creative
thinking skills
Reinforce oral language
by putting it into print
Gain a sense of pride in
writing one's own
version of a story
Create books for a
classroom library
Reinforce grammatical
structures

Class Time
Three or four 45-minute
sessions

Resources
Selections of children's
literature that have a
simple, repetitive, and/
or predictable pattern
(see References and
Further Reading)

Procedure

1. The focus of the activity is to rewrite a story with children, following the original structure of a book with which they are familiar. Begin by reading a children's book that has a simple, repetitive, or predictable pattern:
   - Upon the first reading of the story, point out the title, author, cover illustration, and title page to the children.
   - Encourage discussion and predictions of what the story may be about.
   - Read the story with minimal interruptions so that the children can get a feel for the story in its entirety.
2. Reread the story several times over the next few sessions, each time for a different purpose. Incorporate minilessons on specific skills you may need to cover, such as story content, print concepts, sentence mechanics, vocabulary, phonics, and so on.
3. Write the story on sentence strips, and practice reading from a pocket chart. Cut up the strips into individual words, and have children practice putting them in the correct order.
4. By the 3rd or 4th day, the children should have had enough practice with the original text and should be ready to write their own version of the story:
   - Brainstorm with the children for different ways that the story can be rewritten.
   - Once you come up with an idea, write the new words on sentence strips and replace the original words one at a time. For example, a new version of *Brown Bear, Brown Bear, What Do You See?* (Martin, 1982) can be *Flowers, Flowers, What Do You See?* In this case, replace the *Brown Bear* with *Red Flower* or *Daisy*, with each

subsequent page being a different flower (e.g., *Daisy, Daisy, what do you see? I see a rose looking at me.*). The *What do you see?* throughout the story will remain the same; thus, leave those words in the pocket chart.

5. Once the original words are replaced by the new ones, practice reading the new story from the pocket chart. Give each child one of the sentences to copy and illustrate.

6. When all the pictures are finished, work together with the children to put the pages in the proper order. Allow the children to illustrate the cover as a group, or choose one child to draw it. Make sure that the title page gives credit to the original author and has the names of all the students as illustrators (e.g., *Flowers, Flowers, What Do You See?* Adapted from the story *Brown Bear, Brown Bear, What Do You See?* by Bill Martin, Jr.).

7. Bind the assembled book with a binding machine, if available, or with tape, pipe cleaners, metal rings, string, or garbage bag twist ties.

Caveats and Options

1. If the children are too young to copy the words, circulate around the room and write the words under their pictures as they are drawing.

2. Another version of *Brown Bear* that works well is *Children, Children, What Do You See?* in which each child draws a self-portrait and stands in line with his or her picture. After reciting the words with the children (e.g., *Desi, Desi, what do you see? I see Adam looking at me.*), write the words on the pages and assemble them in the proper order.

3. Use countries of the world or the home countries of your students as other themes for *Brown Bear* (e.g., *United States, United States, what do you see? I see Japan looking at me.*). Continue with other countries, and have students draw their flags. End this version with *I see the world looking at me.* Still other themes are transportation (*Taxi, taxi, what do you see?*) and food groups (*Apple, apple, what do you see?*).

4. Have the children rewrite *Rosie's Walk* (Hutchins, 1983) as their own walk (e.g, *Jake's Walk*), listing all the places they would go. Rewrite *Seven Little Monsters* (Sendak, 1977) to be *Seven Little Children* or *Seven Little Insects* (following a science unit), or change the number

and the adjective (*Ten Humongous Giants*). For *I Was Walking Down the Road* (Barchas, 1988), have the children come up with their own rhymes after a lesson on rhyming. The story's pattern is *I was walking down the road, and I saw a little toad.*

5. Write books based on rewritten versions of popular children's songs. Follow the same procedure as with literature.

6. As you complete more and more books, you will build a classroom library filled with books that the children have completed themselves. In addition, this activity will serve as a springboard for children to begin writing their own original stories.

References and Further Reading

Barchas, S. (1988). *I was walking down the road.* New York: Scholastic.

Carle, E. (1987). *The very hungry caterpillar.* New York: Scholastic.

Hutchins, P. (1983). *Rosie's walk.* New York: Scholastic.

Martin, B., Jr. (1982). *Brown bear, brown bear, what do you see?* Toronto: Holt, Rinehart & Winston.

Sendak, M. (1977). *Seven little monsters.* New York: Harper & Row.

Contributor

Esperanza Saludes Jacobson teaches at Hampton Street Elementary School, Mineola, New York, in the United States.

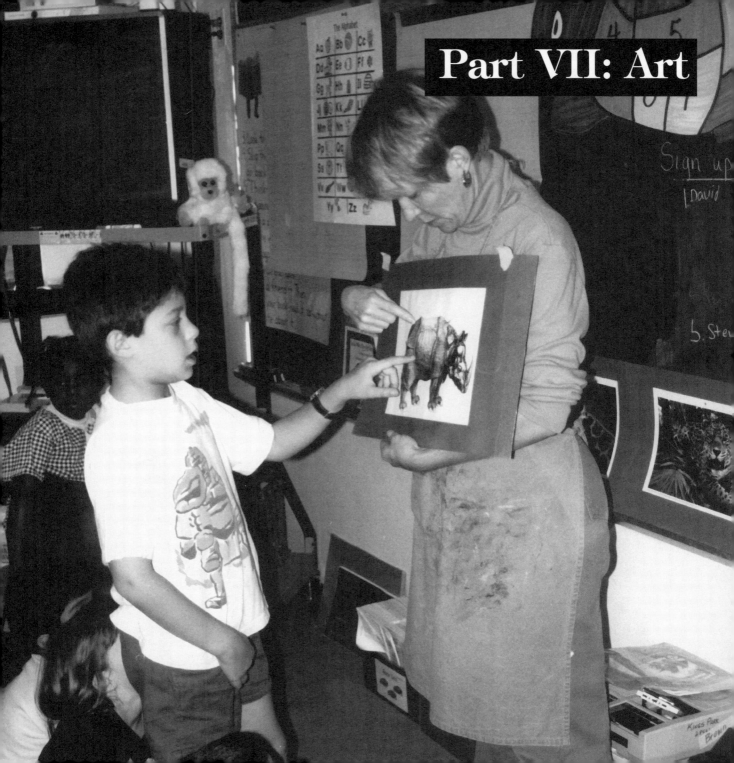

Left to right: Jeffrey Sivek and Peggy Nigon at Kings Park Elementary School, Burke, Virginia, USA.

Word and Sentence Pictures

Levels
Beginning

Aims
Practice new vocabulary
Remember previously
taught vocabulary

Class Time
30–60 minutes

Resources
For each student:
Blank sheet of paper
Crayon
Vocabulary word on a
slip of paper

Procedure

1. Introduce a new group of vocabulary words or review a recently taught group of vocabulary words with the students.
2. Give each student a slip of paper with one of the words on it.
3. Give each student a blank sheet of paper and a crayon.
4. Tell the students to write a sentence at the bottom of their papers using the word they were given. Allow a few minutes for students to make sentences. Help those having trouble.
5. Ask the students to make pictures based on their sentences. For example, if the vocabulary word is *giraffe* and the student's sentence is *I saw a giraffe at the zoo*, the student would draw a giraffe at the zoo. Walk around and assist anyone needing help.
6. Once all the students are finished, have each child stand up and say his or her vocabulary word, read the sentence, and show the picture. Or, if you prefer, collect the papers and put them up around the room to make your own class word-and-sentence art show. Both activities will reinforce the vocabulary words to the other students in the class.

Shawn M. Clankie teaches in Rockton, Illinois, in the United States.

Contributor

Find the Difference

Levels
Intermediate

Aims
Practice asking for
information
Practice giving
information
Practice describing
things based on pictures

Class Time
10–15 minutes

Resources
Pairs of pictures that are
similar but not identical
(e.g., pictures of
animals, birds, flowers,
people, cars, houses,
toys)—one picture per
child

Procedure

1. Divide the class into pairs. Give each child a picture so that the partners have a pair of similar pictures. Tell the children not to look at each other's pictures.
2. Tell the children to ask each other questions to try to find out how many differences there are between their pictures. Model the activity in front of the class if necessary to demonstrate the kind of language they can use.
3. Set a time limit (e.g., 5 minutes). After the time elapses, let the partners compare their pictures.
4. Have the pairs exchange pictures with another pair and start again.

Caveats and Options

For a more elaborate activity, ask pairs to show their pictures to the class and describe the differences (e.g., "We both have birds, but mine is red and his is blue.")

Contributor

Ronald Jackup is a freelance ESL teacher and writer.

Draw the Picture

Levels
Any

Aims
Practice describing
things
Practice using
prepositions of position
Practice listening to
directions

Class Time
15-20 minutes

Resources
Simple drawings or
diagrams for pupils to
describe to a partner

Procedure

1. Divide the class into pairs.
2. Give each pair two different pictures, one for Student A and one for Student B. Tell the children not to look at each other's pictures.
3. Ask Student A to describe his or her picture, and ask B to draw it. B can ask as many questions as necessary but must not look at A's picture. If necessary, model the activity in front of the class before the children begin to demonstrate the kind of language and questions they can use.
4. After 5 minutes, stop the class and ask the children to change roles. Ask B to describe his or her picture for A to draw.
5. After both children have had a chance to draw a picture, have them compare their pictures to the originals.

Contributor

Richard Jacobs is an independent EFL consultant.

Keepsakes

Levels
Beginning–intermediate

Aims
Practice basic question-
and-answer structures
Follow instructions
Get acquainted
Make a keepsake of the
class

Class Time
One class period

Resources
Questionnaire paper
Paper-folding
instructions

Procedure

Stage 1: Class Interview

1. Design a matrix questionnaire appropriate to the level of the students through which they can find out information about each other and practice necessary sentence structures and vocabulary:
   - Write students' names in the left-hand column.
   - Head three or four other columns with key words and phrases for the interview (e.g., *tennis*, *swimming*, *a guitar*) so that students can practice structures like *Do you play/like/have* _____?
   - For more advanced students, head the columns with words and phrases such as *family*, *hobby*, *favorite subject*, and so on so that they can practice *wh-* questions and questions with *how many*.
2. Review and practice the question-and-answer structures required for the interviews, including *How do you spell your name?* and *Could you say it again, please?*
3. Then have students circulate to perform the interviews and fill out their questionnaire forms.

Stage 2: Keepsake Creation

1. Tell the students that they are going to make an interesting shape with their completed questionnaire sheet that will serve as a keepsake of the class.
2. To help them remember this day when they open their paper shape sometime in the future, ask the students to add the date, your name, and the name of the school to the papers.

72

3. Ask the students to fold the paper according to your instructions (see Appendix):
   - Fold the paper in half to create line EF.
   - Fold AB and CD in to EF.
   - Tuck under B along GH. Tuck under D along IJ.
   - Fold back KL horizontally about 2 cm deep.
   - Bring K and L diagonally down until they touch the center EF line, and fold neatly.
   - Bring H and J up until they come to M and N, and then fold.
   - Bring O and P up until they go under G and I, and then fold. You will have a nice-looking shirt in front of you.

Students will get to know each other and learn to work together through this cooperative, high-interest activity, thus generating a positive language learning environment.

Caveats and Options

Appendix: Diagrams for Folding Keepsake Shirt

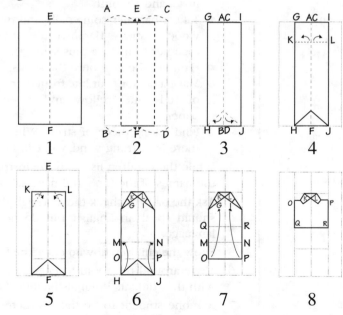

Contributor

Elizabeth Lange teaches at Temple University Japan in Tokyo.

How to Make a Kite

Levels
Beginning

Aims
Practice following
instructions
Review vocabulary for
colors, tools, and
materials
Develop listening
comprehension

Class Time
30-45 minutes

Resources
White and colored
paper
Hammers and nails
Scissors
String
Wooden sticks

Procedure

1. Seat the children in pairs. Distribute the materials for making the kites.
2. Read the following directions or play them on a tape recorder:
   - Take a large piece of paper.
   - Draw a face with two eyes, a big nose, and a mouth.
   - Take a hammer, some nails, and two wooden sticks. Hammer the sticks together to make a plus sign (+).
   - Hammer the face onto the sticks.
   - Make a tail for your kite from pieces of red, blue, yellow, and green paper.
   - Find a long piece of string. When there is a strong wind, you can fly your kite. Good luck!

3. While the children listen to the instructions, have them write down the names of the tools and materials they will need to make a kite.
4. Ask the pairs to check the materials they have against their lists. They should speak in English, but do not forbid the use of the native language.
5. Show the children how to cut a kite face from a piece of white paper.
6. Move around the room to check the students' comprehension. Talk with the students in English about the task.
7. Ask one student to be the instructor. Have the student give orders (e.g., "Hammer the face onto the sticks," "Make a tail for your kite

from pieces of red, blue, yellow, or green paper," or "Find a long piece of string") and ask the other students to fulfill them.

8. When the children have finished their kites, take them out to fly them if possible—or let them test the kites at home and tell each other about their experiences at the next lesson.

Caveats and Options

1. Have the children make their kite faces at home and bring them to school to complete the activity if time does not permit doing the whole activity in the classroom.

2. If children are too young for hammers and nails, have an adult or older student available to help.

Contributor

Eva Tandlichová is a teacher trainer at Comenius University, Bratislava, Slovakia.

Part VIII: Music

Top left to right: David McNiff, Jeffrey Sivek, Steven Diaz, Edward Fuentes. Bottom left to right: Sean Lillard and Lueth Akuak at Kings Park Elementary School, Burke, Virginia, USA.

The Old Lady Who Swallowed a Fly

Levels
Beginning

Aims
Learn farm animal
vocabulary
Identify rhyming words
Use comparatives and
superlatives
Learn sequencing

Class Time
30 minutes

Resources
Figure of the Old Lady
Set of animal pictures
for the teacher and for
each student
Spider made of fuzzy
yarn or pipe cleaners
Recording of the song
"The Old Lady Who
Swallowed a Fly" (the
Burl Ives rendition
works well)
Copies of the words to
the song

Procedure

1. Prior to the lesson, construct a cardboard figure of the Old Lady. My design was based on a pattern from the *Macmillan Early Skills Program* (1983). It is about 25 in. by 12 in. and has a glued-on fabric dress and cotton-ball hair. The stomach is see-through (a vertical rectangle is cut out and replaced with clear plastic). A pocket is glued to the back to hold the animals as they are dropped from behind into the stomach.

2. Also beforehand, draw animals or cut out pictures from books, making certain that the spider is larger than the fly, the bird is larger than the spider, and so forth. Laminate the pictures. As an added attraction, make an extra spider out of fuzzy yarn or pipe cleaners. A string tied to it will allow the students to make it "wiggle" and "jiggle" as the song indicates.

3. Present the Old Lady and the animals to the students, briefly going over their names.

4. Demonstrate *swallow*.

5. Play a recording of the song. Pick up the animals as they are named in the lyrics and have the Old Lady "swallow" them by dropping them into the pocket. They will be seen from the front settling in the stomach.

6. After the first verse, direct different students to "wiggle" and "jiggle" the spider each time it is mentioned.

7. When the initial demonstration is completed, give each student a set of animals. Play the song again, and, as the song is playing, direct individual students to drop in the appropriate animals.

Caveats and Options

1. Have each student construct a smaller, more simplified version of the Old Lady out of oaktag or construction paper. A review of the parts of the body may be incorporated into this activity. Make a fuzzy spider to add to the fun. Evaluate comprehension by observing the students as they listen to the song and manipulate the lady and the animals.
2. Distribute copies of the lyrics. Read them together dramatically. Assign individual students to take the *I don't know why she swallowed the fly* and the *Perhaps she'll die* lines.
3. Give the students felt-tip pens in a variety of colors that may be used as highlighters. Discuss rhyming words, illustrating with the lyrics. Have the students highlight the rhyming sets of words, using a different color for each set.
4. Introduce *first, last, before,* and *after.* Direct the students to hold up the appropriate animal to answer such questions as "What did the Old Lady swallow first?" or "What did she swallow after the cat?"
5. Demonstrate placing the animals in order according to size; the students will do the same with their animals. Introduce the concepts of *bigger, the biggest, smaller, the smallest.*
6. Using pictures, books, and/or manipulatives, present farms and the animals most commonly found on farms. Show examples (pictures or realia) or the work or the products of these animals. Have each student draw a picture of a farm and discuss it.

References and Further Reading

Macmillan Early Skills Program. (1983). New York: Macmillan Educational.

Contributor

Suzan Cole teaches in the Township of Ocean Schools, Ocean, New Jersey, in the United States.

Articles and Reference: Exercises Using Folk Music

Levels
Beginning–intermediate

Aims
Develop accuracy in use
of articles and nominal
reference

Class Time
Five or six sessions of
15–20 minutes per song

Resources
Lyrics to U.S. and
English folk songs
Tape player, compact
disc player, piano, or
guitar
Vocabulary cards

Procedure

1. Obtain written lyrics of a traditional folk song and read the lyrics aloud to the children.
2. Sing or play the melody and then play the full song for the children to hear.
3. Present vocabulary items from the song using picture cards.
4. Discuss the story of the song, asking the children to talk about their ideas.
5. In slow stages, teach the children to sing the song in a group, using considerable repetition.
6. As you teach the song, make the grammatical purposes of the activity explicit. Point out the ways in which articles change in form but not in what they refer to. (Examples: Old MacDonald's farm is first "*a* farm" and then "*that* farm." The Old Lady first swallowed "*a* fly" and then "*the* fly.")
7. Once the children know the song, play a game in which parts of the lyrics (always an article or an article plus a noun) are left out, in cloze style. Have students fill the words in themselves.
8. When appropriate, let the children add nouns of their own to the song in the same format, with the article. Begin by putting new vocabulary on picture cards. Then let students choose their own words to fill in the song.

Caveats and Options

1. If you are not comfortable singing, have older children or a parent lead the singing or rely on recorded versions of the songs.
2. To reinforce the use of articles, play a game that requires internalization in the format of the old camp song, "A Dog Named Bingo": Once a song is familiar, teach the children to leave out more and more of

the lyrics. Use rhythmic clapping to substitute for the missing words, omitting one more word or phrase each time. Finally, have students leave out everything but the articles.

Contributor

Miriam Isaacs is an educational specialist at the COMSIS Mid-Atlantic Multifunctional Resource Center and at the University of Maryland, College Park, Maryland, in the United States.

Body Part Song

Levels
Beginning

Aims
Reinforce understanding
of vocabulary for body
parts
Practice pronunciation
of vocabulary for body
parts

Class Time
10–15 minutes

Resources
None

Procedure

1. To the tune of "I'm a Little Teapot," sing the following words:
   I'm a little body, and my head's on top.
   My feet can run, they never stop.
   My mouth can smile, my hands can clap.
   My eyes can see and blink like that!
   My arms can bend, my nose can smell.
   My fingers can wiggle, my ears as well.
2. Use gestures wherever possible to reinforce vocabulary for body parts and actions.
3. Have the students sing with you, and repeat the song as necessary until all are participating.

Caveats and Options

Have the children create their own lines using the names of other body parts.

Contributor

María A. Martínez teaches at Chappell Elementary School, Chicago, Illinois, in the United States.

Tool Song

Levels
Beginning

Aims
Reinforce understanding
of vocabulary for tools
Practice pronunciation
of vocabulary for tools

Class Time
10–15 minutes

Resources
Real or toy tools

Procedure

1. To the tune of "Mary Had a Little Lamb," sing these words to the children:

   I use a hammer to pound, pound, pound,
   Pound, pound, pound,
   Pound, pound, pound.
   I use a hammer to pound, pound, pound,
   To pound in a nail.
   I use a saw to cut, cut, cut,
   Cut, cut, cut,
   Cut, cut, cut.
   I use a saw to cut, cut, cut,
   To cut a piece of wood.
   (I use a screwdriver to turn, turn, turn . . .
   To turn a screw around.)
   (I use a drill to make a hole, make a hole, make a hole,
   . . . To make a great big hole.)

2. Use real or toy tools to reinforce vocabulary as you sing.
3. Sing with the children, and repeat the song until all are involved.

Caveats and Options

Have the children create their own lines using the names of other tools.

Contributor

María A. Martínez teaches at Chappell Elementary School, Chicago, Illinois, in the United States.

Vehicle Song

Levels
Beginning

Aims
Reinforce understanding
of vocabulary for
vehicles
Practice pronunciation
of vocabulary for
vehicles

Class Time
10-15 minutes

Resources
Vehicle pictures or
objects

Caveats and Options

Contributor

Procedure

1. To the tune of "Mary Had a Little Lamb," sing the following to the class:

   > The boat floats in the water, in the water, in the water.
   > The boat floats in the water—toot, toot, toot!
   > The shiny car drives on the road, on the road, on the road.
   > The shiny car drives on the road—beep, beep, beep!
   > The airplane flies in the sky, in the sky, in the sky.
   > The airplane flies in the sky—zoom, zoom, zoom!
   > The circus train goes on the tracks, on the tracks, on the tracks.
   > The circus train goes on the tracks—choo, choo, choo!

2. Use objects or pictures to illustrate each vehicle as you sing.
3. Have the children join with you and repeat the song until all are involved.

Have the children create lines with names of other vehicles, such as truck or bus.

María A. Martínez teaches at Chappell Elementary School, Chicago, Illinois, in the United States.

Where Do I Wear It?

Levels
Beginning

Aims
Reinforce understanding
of vocabulary for
clothing
Practice pronunciation
of vocabulary for
clothing

Class Time
10–15 minutes

Resources
None

Caveats and Options

Contributor

Procedure

1. Have the students stand in a circle.

2. Using appropriate gestures, sing the following with the children to the tune of "The Farmer in the Dell":

    The shirt goes on my arms.
    The shirt goes on my arms.
    Hi, ho, when I get dressed,
    The shirt goes on my arms.

3. Continue with these verses:

    The pants go on my legs.
    The socks go on my feet.
    The shoes go on my feet.
    The hat goes on my head.
    The mittens go on my hands.

Have the children create their own verses using the names of other clothing items.

María A. Martínez teaches at Chappell Elementary School, Chicago, Illinois, in the United States.

Class Cassette

Levels
Any

Aims
Reinforce songs and
language already studied
Listen to a recording at
home for further
reinforcement

Class Time
Parts of several class
periods

Resources
Cassette player
Cassette tape for each
student

Procedure

1. Plan the number of songs you wish to record and the order of the recordings. These should be songs the students have already learned.
2. Plan introductions and speaking, singing, and sound effects parts for all the students. You might have them say their name and favorite thing at the beginning: "I'm Juan, and I like bicycles." Depending on their ability and how many students you have, you may wish to give each one "center stage" at least once during the recordings. Advanced students can sing the more lengthy songs with lots of words; those in the lower levels can say short phrases for introductions and participate in the Total Physical Response songs.
3. Design or have students design cassette inserts. Make enough photocopies so that each student will have one.
4. Record the collection of songs with your students. Recording several sessions of the same material allows you to choose the selections that worked out well and then mix them onto a master tape.
5. After recording, make cassette copies (with the aid of a language lab technician, if necessary) for each student. Record a personal message to each student if there is enough room at the end of each cassette.
6. Distribute the cassettes and have the students color the cassette inserts and add their names.

Caveats and Options

1. With more advanced students, do this activity with popular songs that they like to sing.
2. Include other things on the cassette, such as a funny short story, jokes, and interviews.

3. Make the recording like a radio show with a mixture of songs, publicity spots, interviews, and disc-jockey chatter.
4. With the students or by yourself, create a booklet to go along with the cassette.

Contributor

Tim Murphey teaches at Nanzan University, Nagoya, Japan.

Class Songbooklet

Levels
Any

Aims
Reinforce songs and
language studied
Create a songbook for
the classroom or for
individual use

Class Time
Throughout the term

Resources
Copies of selected song
lyrics for each student

Procedure

1. Choose several songs to teach the children. Copy and collate the lyrics at the beginning of the term.
2. Work through the songs during the term, allowing the children to write the lyrics they sing and to color the lyric sheets as you go.
3. Have the children gather all the songs into a book and decorate the cover.

Caveats and Options

1. Instead of individual booklets, make a class song folder in which to put copies of songs from you or songs written in the students' own hands. At the end of the term, help the students put the songs into a more permanent form with a cover page.
2. Near the end of the term, give the students the written lyrics of the songs that you have taught orally during the term. Ideally, they should have time to sing through each song a few times to get used to reading it. They can also add their individual touches of color and drawing.
3. Have the class record all or some of the songs on a cassette.
4. Compile songbooks for special occasions like holidays, for a school play, or around a theme.
5. Give the students parts of the songs and have them fill in missing words, lines, or verses.
6. Be sure not to use copyrighted material without permission.

Contributor

Tim Murphey teaches at Nanzan University, Nagoya, Japan.

Part IX: Drama

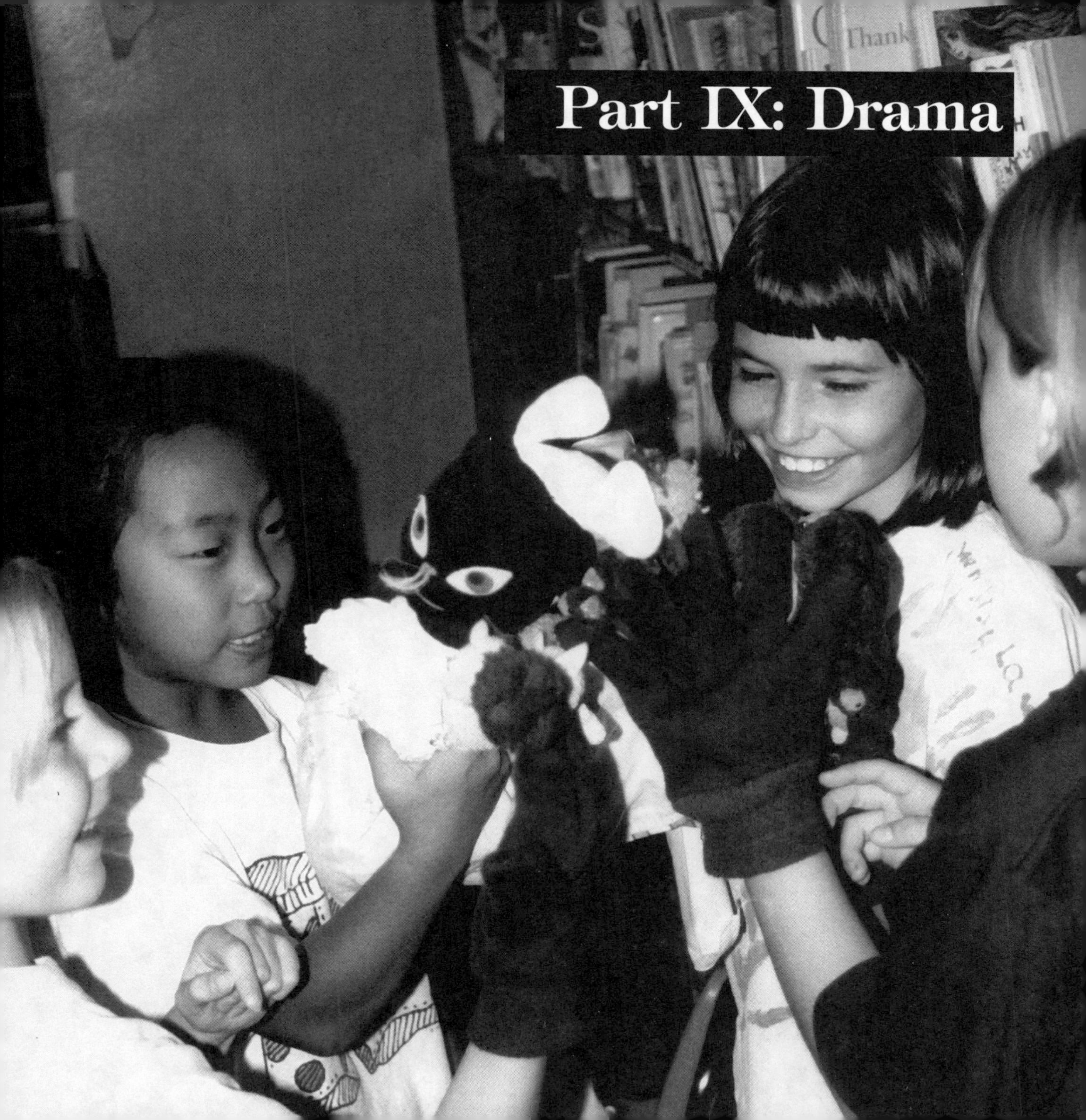

Left to right: Elaine Kopko, Hye-Yoon Chung, and Jennifer Bergeron at Kings Park Elementary School, Burke, Virginia, USA.

In-Character Play as Practice of Conversation Skills

Levels
Beginning

Aims
Practice conversation skills in a familiar doll-play setting

Class Time
15 minutes once or twice a week

Resources
Small dolls and stuffed animals
Doll house furniture
Clothes, cars, and other props for dolls

Procedure

1. Divide the class into pairs or groups of three.
2. Introduce the dolls to the children as if the dolls themselves were speaking. The dolls are "monolingual English speakers."
3. Divide the toys by lottery. Distribute the dolls and props so that each child has at least one doll to operate.
4. Let each group improvise play with the dolls, speaking in "the dolls' voices." Because the dolls can speak only English, the children will have a natural reason to practice their conversation skills.
5. Rotate the dolls so that each group gets to play with the favorites.

Contributor

Helena Halmari teaches at Sam Houston State University, Huntsville, Texas, in the United States.

What Is She Doing?

Levels
Beginning

Aims
Practice the present
continuous tense of
action verbs

Class Time
5–10 minutes

Resources
None

Procedure

1. Have the children stand in a circle.
2. Call one child aside and whisper an instruction for him or her to mime in the center of the circle (e.g, *wash your hair*).
3. Tell the other children to walk around in a circle asking "What's Laura doing?" while the child mimes the action.
4. Ask someone to guess what Laura is doing. If the guess is correct, have the two children change places. If the guess is not correct, the game continues.

Contributor

Richard Jacobs is an independent EFL consultant.

Mirror Mime

Levels
Beginning–intermediate

Aims
Practice using regular
and irregular past-tense
verb forms
Practice using
sequencers

Class Time
15 minutes

Resources
None

Procedure

1. Have pairs of children stand facing each other.
2. Direct one student in each pair to mime a series of four actions (e.g., brushing teeth, combing hair, peeling a banana, looking at a watch). The other students must follow their partners' actions as closely as possible, as if they are mirror images.
3. After 5 minutes, ask one pair to perform its mirror mime in front of the class.
4. When the short mime is over, ask the class to tell what actions the pair mimed. Have them use the past tense and link their statements with *first*, *then*, *then*, and *and then*. ("First he brushed his teeth. Then he combed his hair. Then he peeled a banana. And then he looked at his watch.")

Caveats and Options

1. Before playing the Mirror Mime game, write a list of base verb forms on the board (e.g., *brush*, *look*, *clean*, *wash*, *fall asleep*, *eat*). Then elicit the past-tense form of each verb. These verbs will act as prompts for preparing mirror mimes and also for describing the mimes.
2. After one pair has performed its mirror mime for the class, write four verbs on the board that correspond to the actions of that mime. The verbs should be written out of order. Then ask the class to tell the correct order of the mimed actions, using *first*, *then*, *then*, and *and then*.
3. Ask the students to write a description of one of the mimes for written reinforcement.

Contributor

Dino Mahoney teaches at the City University of Hong Kong.

Noah's Ark

Levels
Beginning

Aims
Practice vocabulary for names of animals

Class Time
10 minutes

Resources
Index cards (one per student)
Colored pens or markers
Adhesive tape

Procedure

1. Using different-colored pens or markers, write each animal name (e.g., elephant, snake, giraffe, chimpanzee) on two different cards.
2. Stick a card on each child's back without showing it to him or her. Ask the children not to tell each other what their cards say.
3. Have the children circulate, pairing up and miming the name of the animal on their partner's back.
4. Once the children have guessed their animal names, tell them to find the other student wearing the same name—again, by miming the animal rather than by talking.

Caveats and Options

1. Repeat the game by changing the cards on the children's backs.
2. Play the game at higher levels using facial expressions. Draw faces on the cards to represent moods (e.g., happy, sad, angry, sleepy, grumpy, dreamy, thoughtful) and have the children circulate, miming the expressions and finding the other child with the same mood as theirs.

Contributor

Dino Mahoney teaches at the City University of Hong Kong.

Part X: Storytelling

Left to right: Maryam Sodeifi and Meena Na at Kings Park Elementary School, Burke, Virginia, USA.

Picture Stories

Levels
Intermediate

Aims
Practice storytelling
Practice listening to a story
Practice creative thinking

Class Time
10–15 minutes

Resources
Two objects or pictures of objects per student (e.g., small household items or magazine pictures of interesting, unusual, or familiar items)

Contributor

Procedure

1. Divide the class into groups of four or five. Give each child two items or pictures.
2. Tell each group the first sentence of a story (e.g., *Yesterday after school I took the bus downtown.*).
3. Have each group member continue the story, using one of his or her items or pictures. For example, a child with a picture of a car might say, "I wanted to buy a toy car for my sister."
4. Continue the game until each group member has had two turns. The challenge is to make the story as interesting or as funny as possible.
5. Let each group tell its story to the class.

Caveats and Options

1. Have the children write out their stories as a follow-up activity.
2. Change the activity to a written activity by giving each group a piece of paper to pass around. The students take turns writing out sentences to add to the story.

Ronald Jackup is a freelance EFL teacher and writer.

Telling Tales

Levels
Intermediate

Aims
Integrate listening, speaking, reading, and writing in a comparison/contrast unit using traditional tales

Class Time
A month-long unit

Resources
Books of fairy tales, folktales, and fables
Two versions of a particular tale

Procedure

1. Tell the students a tale that comes from your cultural heritage.
2. Tell students that they must tell a tale to their classmates:
   - Instruct them to go home and discuss their cultural heritage with their parents and to have their parents tell or read them a tale from that background.
   - Encourage them to practice telling the tale that they choose by using their family as the audience.
   - Have two or three students per day tell their tales to the class.
3. Continue to read and tell a variety of traditional tales throughout the unit. Have books in the classroom to reflect the theme so that when the students have silent reading time, they can choose books that are consistent with the theme.
4. When the students begin to see similarities and differences between their tales and the ones that their classmates are telling,
   - Discuss the terms *compare* and *contrast*.
   - Have students orally compare and contrast objects they are familiar with.
   - Have the students identify words and phrases that indicate that a comparison or a contrast is taking place (e.g., *in addition, furthermore,* and *on the other hand*). Develop a list of these words that can be posted in the classroom.
   - Have students attempt to write a comparison/contrast paragraph.
5. Within the context of the storytelling, develop vocabulary. In addition, have students start acquiring stylistic conventions that are often found in traditional tales, such as a standard beginning, repetition of language, repetition of events, flat characterizations, and moralistic endings.

6. Use two versions of a traditional tale for the culminating activity:
   - Divide the class in two, and have each half read one version.
   - Pair up the students who read Version 1 with those who read Version 2.
   - Have each member of the pair tell (not read) his or her version to the other.
   - Have the partners jointly make a list of similarities and differences between the versions.
   - Reconvene the class and open the discussion of similarities and differences to the class as a whole. Keep a chart of the comments made.
7. Finally, have students write a comparison/contrast composition using the two versions of the tale. The chart and previous lists made will be helpful at this time.

Caveats and Options

Have pairs of students brainstorm an idea for a traditional tale. Then have the partners split up and write their own versions, using the same ideas but creating their own details. When they finish, have the partners compare and contrast their stories.

Contributor

Sharon Kennedy teaches at Jakarta International School, Jakarta, Indonesia.

Draw and Tell

Levels
Beginning–intermediate

Aims
Reinforce the use of
prepositions
Practice storytelling

Class Time
20 minutes

Resources
Easel paper and marker
or chalkboard and chalk
Paper and pencils for
students

Procedure

1. Before class, sketch a simple living room scene on the easel paper or chalkboard.
2. When the children arrive, begin adding animals to the picture. Ask the children to name each thing you draw.
3. Explain that you are going to tell a story about the picture, and invite the students to help. ("There's a cat sleeping on the sofa, and there's something under the rug. What is it? Yes, it's very small. No, it's not an ant. Yes, it's a mouse. Oh, no! What do you think will happen?")

4. Guide the children in telling the story: "Where does the mouse run?" (under the table). "What happens next?" "What does the cat do?"

5. Draw a duplicate living room and move the animals to their new places in the story. Continue and demonstrate on the sketch: "The mouse runs under the cord, the cat jumps over the cord, the lamp falls on the floor and breaks into many pieces . . . ."

6. Then ask the big question: "Does the cat catch the mouse?" Finish the story: "Where can the mouse go to be safe? Under the rug again? No. Under the sofa? Yes. And what does the cat do? He goes back to sleep on the sofa."

7. Give each of the children a piece of paper and a pencil. Ask them to draw their own pictures to retell all or part of the story. Walk around the room to comment and ask questions, such as "I see the mouse running under the sofa, but where is the cat?" or "Oh, the mouse isn't hiding under the rug. He's sitting on the rug."

Caveats and Options

1. This activity is limited only by your imagination and your artistic skills—but let me emphasize that my artistic skills are not very advanced. My students often enjoy a laugh at my expense when they misinterpret my drawings. I feel a little embarrassment is worthwhile as I'm asking my students to display an imperfect skill, and my risk taking seems to encourage theirs.

2. Use this technique to tell anecdotes about things that have happened to you, events you have read about in the newspaper, or stories you have read in class.

Contributor

Alison Williams teaches in the Three Village Central School District and at Suffolk Community College, Long Island, New York, in the United States.

Time—People—Action—Place

Levels
Beginning

Aims
Practice using the past
tense accurately
Practice constructing
simple sentences

Class Time
10–15 minutes

Resources
None

Procedure

1. Divide the class into four groups.
2. Have each group be responsible for one category: Time, People, Action, Place. After a few rounds, the groups can exchange categories.
3. Tell each group to discuss among themselves what they will choose to express their category. Remind the Time and Action groups to choose past time markers and verbs in the past form. For example:

   Time group: *yesterday morning*
   People group: *our teacher, Mr. Chan*
   Action group: *snored loudly*
   Place group: *in the office*

4. Instruct students to make a complete sentence using the phrases chosen (e.g., *Yesterday morning our teacher, Mr. Chan, snored loudly in the office.*).
5. Write down the finished sentence on the board for discussion. Explain, if necessary, cases when the past continuous tense should have been used—for instance, when the Time group chooses a marker such as *at ten o'clock last night.*
6. Repeat the same procedure a few times. Students can make as many sentences as they like.
7. Remind students that the same sentence can be expressed in a slightly different way when the word order is changed. That is, the Time group can be put at the end of the round. In the case of this example, the sentence would read *Our teacher, Mr. Chan, snored loudly in the office yesterday morning.*

Caveats and Options

1. This activity is appropriate for consolidating rather than introducing language structures.
2. This activity will open a lot of possibilities, and students will probably make humorous or even nonsense sentences as the four groups prepare their own items without knowing what the other groups will choose.

Contributor

Matilda M. W. Wong teaches at the City University of Hong Kong.

Part XI: Writing

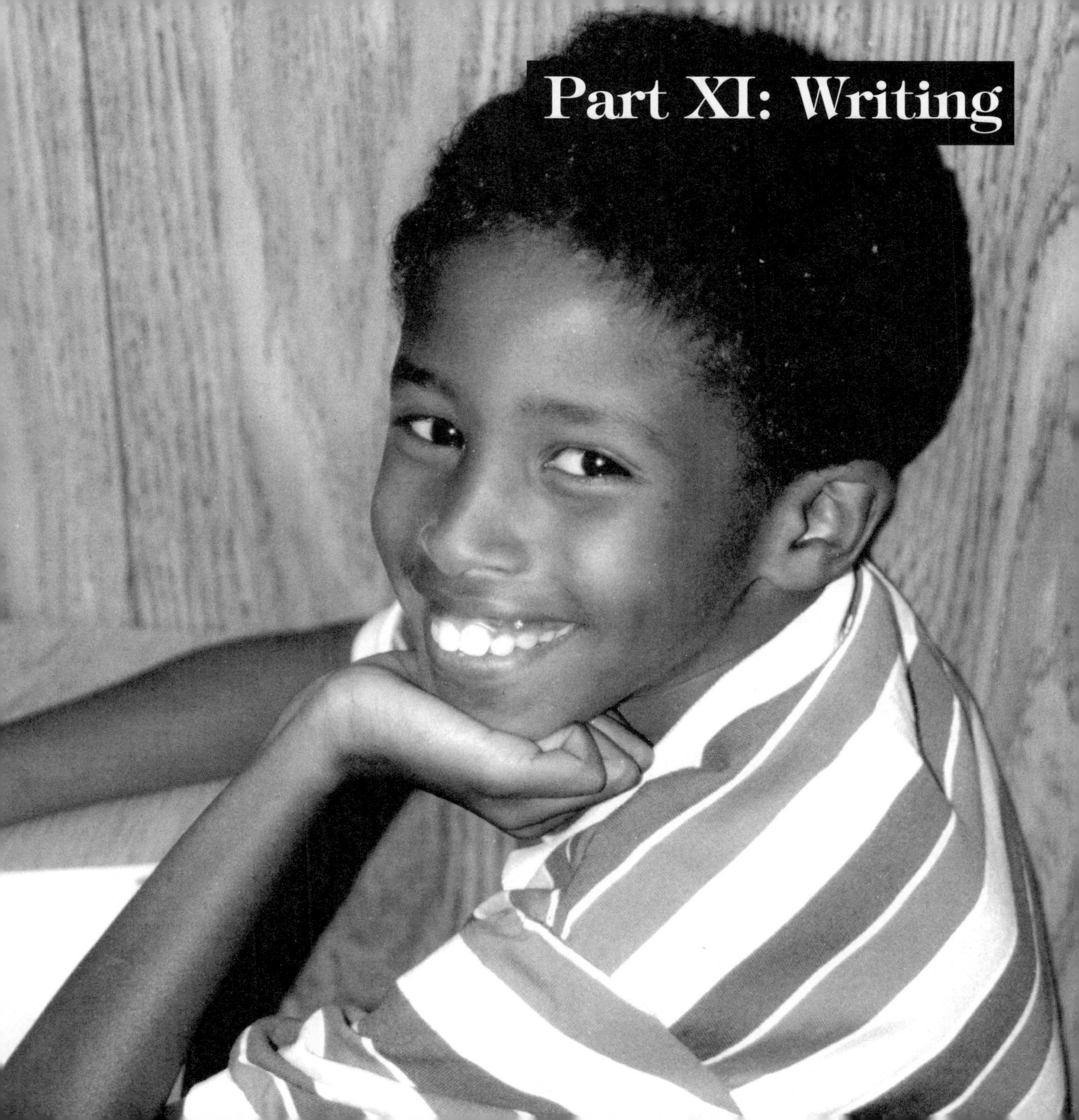

Left to right: Mohamud Mohamud at Kings Park Elementary School, Burke, Virginia, USA.

Choose Your Words

Levels
Beginning–intermediate

Aims
Create sentences
Practice word order

Class Time
20–30 minutes

Resources
One grid per group
with nouns, adjectives,
and numbers to practice
(see Appendix A)
Blank paper for each
student

Procedure

1. Prepare the grid and make one copy for each group.
2. Divide the class into groups of three to five students.
3. Distribute the grids and blank sheets of paper, and let the students discuss the words.
4. Explain the rules:
   - As a group, order the words in a sentence, and write it on the piece of paper. Use as many words as you can. Use them in any order, but don't repeat any.
   - Add as many words as needed to complete the sentence (e.g., *Ten books were under the picture.*).
5. Once the groups have created their sentences, have them exchange papers to review others' sentences.

Caveats and Options

1. For older or intermediate English students, change the words in the grid, and have the students create more elaborate sentences or require students to use a certain number of words from the grid. An example is *Some very important documents were lost (found) in the street some days ago.* (See Appendix B.)
2. Have students work individually instead of in small groups.

Appendix A: Sample Grid for Beginning Students

blue	ten	books
picture	red	blackboard
one	pen	green

Appendix B: Sample Grid for Intermediate Students

impossible	documents	lost
to find	important	in
the street	days ago	some

Contributor

Teresa Deagostini teaches at Colegio Jean Piaget and Crandon Institute, Montevideo, Uruguay.

Jigsaw Puzzle Writing

Levels
Beginning-low
intermediate

Aims
Review spelling of
vocabulary words
Write complete
sentences
Practice creative
storytelling
Practice using
vocabulary words in
natural conversation

Class Time
20-30 minutes

Resources
Jigsaw puzzle of a scene
related to the
vocabulary topic

Contributor

Procedure

1. Set up a jigsaw puzzle on a side table. Use a large piece of cardboard for ease of storing and moving. Tape the sides to prevent losing pieces.
2. Start out by letting students work on the puzzle when they have extra time or during recess. Use this time for natural conversation about items in the puzzle, thus reinforcing vocabulary.
3. After the puzzle is complete, ask each of the students to look at the picture and to think of a sentence about it.
4. Have students take turns writing the sentences on the board while others copy them. Discuss spelling and mechanics as they occur in the sentences.

Caveats and Options

1. Ask students to form sentences that will make an ongoing story.
2. This is a good activity for multilevel classes. All students can share in working on the puzzle, and students' sentences can vary in difficulty even within one class.

Joan Dungey is an educational consultant in Yellow Springs, Ohio, in the United States.

Convince Me

Levels
Intermediate +

Aims
Improve expository
skills in writing
academic English
See writing as a more
social experience
Increase computer
fluency

Class Time
One class period, then
10 minutes out of each
computer writing period
throughout the term or
year

Resources
Computer for each child
or pair of children
Computer disk for each
child

Procedure

1. Provoke an oral argument or two in class (e.g., say, "We should wear uniforms in school." or "We need more time for art."), trying to stir up a heated debate. Write the students' comments on the board.
2. Introduce the rules of the activity:
   - At the beginning of each computer writing period, before starting on their writing, students should call up an ongoing argument file.
   - They should enter the date and their name.
   - Students should then respond to the teacher's last comment (entered since their last entry).
   - They should try to win the argument (i.e., convince the teacher they are right) using reasoning, experiences, and analogies.
   - They can start a new argument (file) or add to an old one, but the teacher may instruct students which file to work on.
3. The following day, hand students their own disks with your first argument entered.
4. Give them 10 minutes to write their entry.
5. Record the winning points on a class chart.

112

Caveats and Options

1. Have the children work in pairs at the computer, discuss the pros and cons of an argument, and decide on a joint response.
2. If several of the debates lag, switch the disks around and have students make entries in other students' arguments.

Contributor

Jacqueline Leigh is a librarian and ESL teacher at the American International School of Freetown in Sierra Leone.

Get-Acquainted Books

Levels
Beginning

Aims
Practice communication
skills during a language
experience activity

Class Time
20–30 minutes daily for
8 days

Resources
Camera (preferably
instant-developing)
Crayons
Glue sticks
Paper for book pages
Sentence strips for
books (see Appendix)

Procedure

1. Day 1: Have students complete Sentence Strip 1 and use a *glue stick* to put it on a book *page*. Have students draw a picture of themselves on the page and practice reading the completed page.
2. Day 2: Walk around the school inside and outside. Point out names of places and things. Have students complete Strip 2 and glue it on a page. Have them draw a picture of the school on the page and practice reading pages 1 and 2.
3. Day 3: Take a picture of each student with his or her homeroom teacher. Have students complete Sentence 3 and glue it on a page. Ask them to glue the picture to the *center* of the page. Have students practice reading pages one, two, and three, emphasizing such phrases as *first page*, *turn the page*, and so on.
4. Day 4: Visit the principal in his or her office, and take a picture of each student with the principal. Have students complete Sentence Strip 4 and glue it on a page. Ask them to put the picture in the center of the page and practice reading pages 1–4 as you did on Day 3.
5. Days 5, 6, and 7: Visit each additional teacher (art, music, gym) and take a picture of each student with the teacher. Have the students complete a sentence strip for each and glue the strips and photos to additional pages. Continue to have students practice reading each page.
6. Day 8: Invite students to make a *cover* for their books and to assemble them. Have students read their books several times and take them home to share with family.

Caveats and Options

1. For Days 5, 6, and 7, add labeled pictures to the pages. For example, add brushes, scissors, and paints to the art page; notes and instruments to the music page; and balls and basketball nets to the gym page.
2. Italicized words are examples of the many terms that can be stressed during this activity.
3. This activity can be used with any ages and grades.
4. Parents are especially delighted when the students bring home the books and read them to their families.

Appendix: Sentence Strips

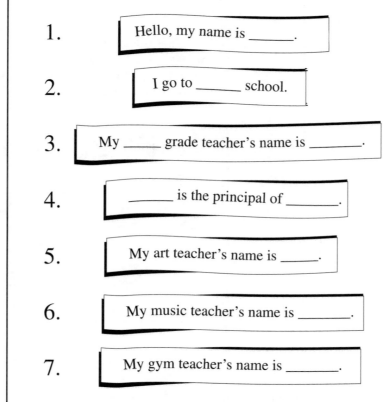

1. Hello, my name is _____.

2. I go to _____ school.

3. My _____ grade teacher's name is _____.

4. _____ is the principal of _____.

5. My art teacher's name is _____.

6. My music teacher's name is _____.

7. My gym teacher's name is _____.

Contributor

Suzanne Robbins is a general education resource teacher in the Bloomfield Hills Public Schools, West Bloomfield, Michigan, in the United States.

Writing a School Newspaper

Levels
Beginning-intermediate

Aims
Use all forms of English
usage in real situations
Practice process writing
in authentic situations
Write in English for
communication
purposes
Become involved in the
school and community

Class Time
Variable

Resources
Newspaper
Typewriter or computer
with word processing
program
Copy machine
Paper

Procedure

1. Introduce the local newspaper. Point out the various sections such as news, sports, movie reviews, and so on.
2. Announce that the class will be making a school newspaper. Have students work individually or in groups to choose the section of the school newspaper that they would like to write.
3. Instruct students on the procedures for conducting interviews, gathering news, or drawing cartoons.

4. Supervise the students' transformation of raw data into a written rough draft.
5. Assign a team of editors to proofread the drafts. Membership on this team should rotate among the students.

6. As students revise their drafts and produce their final copies, have them use a newspaper or newsletter format.
7. Publish enough copies so that each classroom in the school has access to the newspaper.

Caveats and Options

1. Suggested sections of the newspaper are school news, school sports updates, interviews with school personnel, community news, cafeteria food reviews, a puzzle page, poetry, movie and television reviews, and comics (this is especially good for beginning students).
2. Request copying funds from the school parent-teacher organization or from a community group, and publish enough copies for each student in the school to have one.

Contributor

Jo Ann Robisheaux teaches at Jefferson Parish Public Schools, Harvey, Louisiana, in the United States.

Once Upon a Time

Levels
Beginning-low
intermediate

Aims
Practice creative writing

Class Time
30 minutes

Resources
Fairy tale in the format
of a cloze worksheet
(see Appendix)
Enough copies of the
worksheet for each
student

Procedure

1. Divide the class into small groups of two or three, or address the whole class to allow for individual work.
2. Explain the task to students: They have to expand the given text by completing the blanks in the passage. They can create the story in any way they like.
3. Before they begin writing, have students brainstorm for possible ideas and vocabulary to use.
4. At the end of the writing, ask groups or individuals to volunteer to read their stories.
5. Have students illustrate their stories and display them around the room, or collect them in a class book.

Caveats and Options

For smaller classes (of 16 or fewer students), turn the activity into a competition:

1. Write the structure of the story twice, on the left and on the right of the blackboard.
2. Divide the class into two groups.
3. Have group members take turns completing the story by sending a different representative to fill in each blank in the structure.
4. Compare the two versions to select the funnier, scarier, or more unusual one. (For low-intermediate learners, brainstorm on selection criteria as additional oral work.)

Appendix: Sample Fairy Tale

Complete the following story in any way you wish:

Once upon a time, there was _____ who lived _____ with _____.

They were all very _____, and every day _____. One day a _____

witch came to _____. Everyone was _____ about this, and they all

_____.

Suddenly, _____. The witch _____, and they _____. Finally,

_____, and _____ was dead. When they saw that _____ was

dead, _____. And they lived _____ ever after.

Contributor

Wai-king Tsang teaches at the City University of Hong Kong.

Part XII: Content Areas

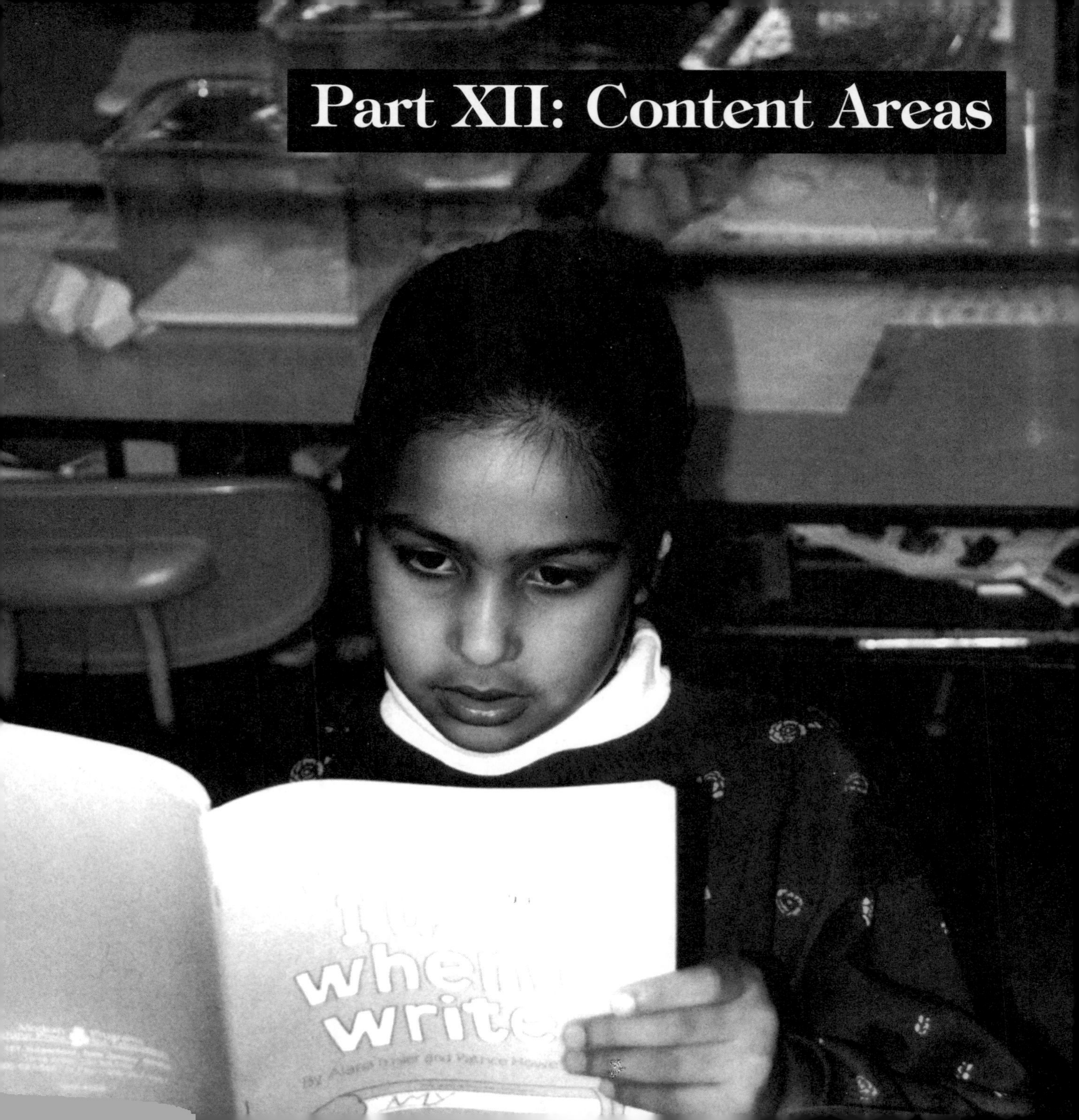

Amarpreet Ghuman at Kings Park Elementary School, Burke, Virginia, USA.

ESL Math

Levels
Intermediate

Aims
Develop the concept of
liquid measurements
(e.g., ounce, pint, quart)
Practice past tense of
regular verbs

Class Time
20 minutes

Resources
8-oz glass
Pint pitcher
Quart pitcher
Gallon pitcher

Procedure

1. Teach or review the following vocabulary: *poured*, *filled*, *glass*, *pitcher*, *ounce*, *pint*, *quart*, *gallon*.
2. Ask a student to fill the glass with water. Then ask him or her to pour the water into a pitcher. Ask the student what he or she did. (For example, elicit, "I filled the glass with water. I poured the water into the pitcher.")
3. Have the student call on another to repeat the process.
4. Write on the board the sentences with *filled* and *poured* after several students have had a chance to fill and pour.
5. Now have a student fill a pitcher with two glasses of water. Say, "You poured a pint of water. What did you pour?" and "You filled the pitcher with a pint of water. What did you fill?"
6. Give other students a turn and continue with
   4 glasses and 16 glasses.
   Vary with 2 pints, 4 quarts,
   and so on.

123

Caveats and Options

1. Have students draw 8-oz glasses and pint, quart, and gallon pitchers for comparison. Then have them make a list of liquids and put them under the headings *glass*, *pint*, *quart*, and *gallon*.
2. For older, more advanced students, include a discussion of ounces and liters.
3. This activity appears in *Project Masters* (1983).

References and Further Reading

Project Masters. (1983). Brooklyn, NY: Brooklyn, NY, school district.

Contributor

Lawrence Fleck teaches at P. S. 212, Brooklyn, New York, in the United States.

Fun With Numbers

Levels
Beginning-low
intermediate

Aims
Practice listening to
numbers
Practice reading
numbers

Class Time
15-20 minutes

Resources
Copies of a grid with
numbers 1-50 (see
Appendix A)

Procedure

1. Create a grid with numbers 1-50. (See Appendix A.) Photocopy about 10 copies of the grid for each child in the class.
2. Before class, decide on pictures you can create by joining the numbers vertically, horizontally, or diagonally. (See Appendix B for an example.)
3. Have the children listen and, with a pencil or crayon, join the numbers you call out. Then let the children tell you what the picture is.
4. Repeat the procedure with two or three more pictures. (See Appendix C.)
5. Have children see what other pictures they can create by working in pairs or small groups. Without showing their work to other pairs or groups, have them tell the others how to form more pictures.

Caveats and Options

1. Vary the pictures by placing some of them on a slant.
2. Increase the grid to 100 numbers to make possible more complicated pictures and thus more language.
3. Use a grid with letters for forming words.

Appendix A:
Grid

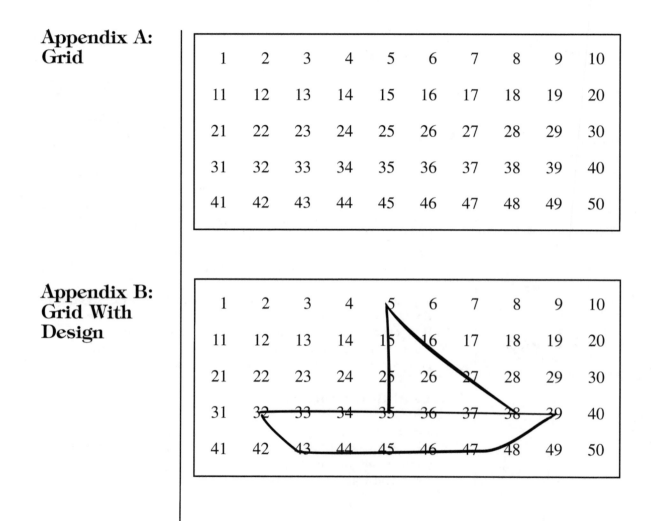

Appendix B:
Grid With
Design

Appendix C: Suggestions for Other Pictures

Join the numbers as follows:

House: 4, 5, 6, 7; 22, 13, 4; 7, 18, 29; 22, 23, 24, 25, 26, 27, 28, 29; 23, 33, 43; 28, 38, 48

Table (on a slant): 7, 8, 9; 23, 15, 7; 25, 17, 9; 23, 24, 25; 23, 33, 43; 25, 35, 45; 9, 19, 29; 17, 27

Box: as for table, except remove 17, 27. Replace with 45, 37, 29; 43, 44, 45.

Contributor

Hyacinth Gaudart teaches at the University of Malaya, Kuala Lumpur, Malaysia.

A Grid Map Comes Alive

Levels
Beginning

Aims
Practice reading and
pronouncing words that
identify buildings found
within a community
Practice constructing
and reading a grid map

Class Time
30–40 minutes

Resources
Yarn
Masking tape
Cards lettered A, B, C,
D, E, F, G, H (one letter
per card)
Cards numbered 1, 2, 3,
4, 5, 6, 7, 8 (one
number per card)
Labeled picture cards of
buildings in a
community
Grid map key (see
Appendix C)

Procedure

1. Prior to the arrival of the class, construct a grid map on the floor of the classroom using yarn and masking tape. (See Appendix A.)
2. Seat the children around the grid map outline.
3. Distribute the letter and number cards. Have the children place the cards next to the grid outline in the appropriate places. (See Appendix B.)
4. Present the labeled picture cards. Read each card aloud and have the children pronounce each word. Give each card to a different child.
5. Present the map key (see Appendix C), read through it while the children follow along, and prominently display it.
6. Have the children with cards take turns placing themselves on the grid map according to the information provided in the map key. The children must announce their building name and location as they take their places on the map. The children are responsible for checking each other for accuracy.
7. Ask the children to take turns calling out building names and placements for additional practice. Make sure that each child has a chance to hold a card and find a place on the grid map.

Caveats and Options

If space is limited, use a game board-sized grid map and have the players place picture cards directly on the grid map.

Appendix A: Grid Map Outline

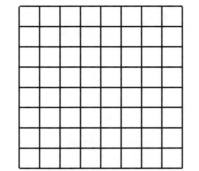

Appendix B: Grid Map Outline With Numbers and Letters

Appendix C: Grid Map Key

Library	H-5
Police Station	B-2
School	F-8
Post Office	A-7
Bank	C-4
Supermarket	A-1
Fire Station	D-3
Town Hall	E-6
Shopping Mall	G-3
Gas Station	C-8

Contributor

Anne Grewe teaches at East Brook Middle School, Paramus, New Jersey, in the United States.

Content Area Picture Books

Levels
Beginning +

Aims
Learn about a particular topic, in this case bears
Make a class book on that topic

Class Time
Three to five 45-minute sessions

Resources
Several books, magazine articles, and pictures on bears (or a topic of your choice)

Procedure

1. Begin the unit/lesson by making a KWL chart about bears with the students (what they *k*now, what they *w*ant to learn, and later what they have *l*earned). Elicit ways that the children could find out things in the want-to-learn column (e.g., library, encyclopedia, books, magazines, experts in the field). Help them to find the information they want to learn.
2. Read the children some stories about bears that are fiction (e.g., *Goldilocks and the Three Bears*) and some that are more informative in nature.
3. For young children, make a Fact/Fiction chart and compare the things that are real about bears and the things that are not.
4. Fill in the KWL chart with the things the children have learned.
5. Make a web to illustrate the findings. (See Appendix A.)
6. Make sentences from the web, and have each child pick a sentence to illustrate for a class book. (See Appendix B.)
7. Have more advanced learners write up a research project. (See Appendix C.)

Caveats and Options

1. This lesson lends itself very well to the study of animals. However, many other content areas can be used, such as science (magnets, electricity, weather, clouds), social studies (community workers, countries), art (artists, movements), and music (instruments, composers).
2. If you are using animals as the topic, group two or three children together and have each group research a different animal. After the children are finished, they can all come together to share what they have learned about each animal.

Appendix A: Sample *Bears* Web

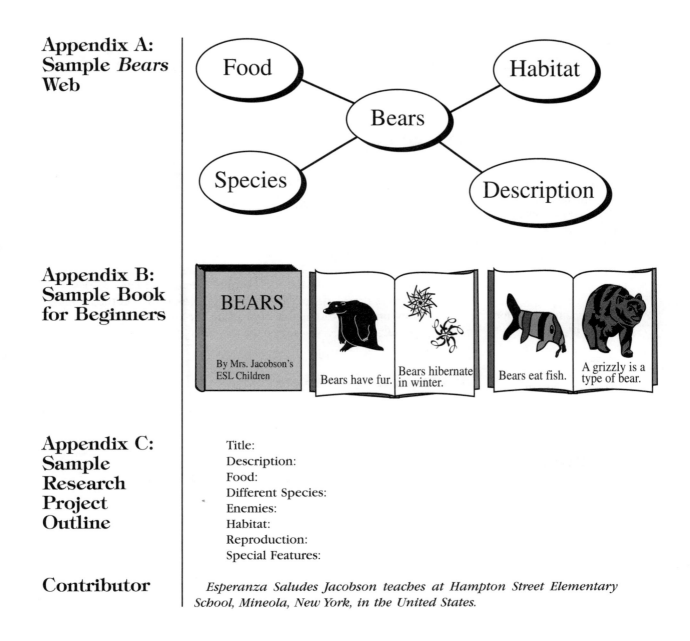

Appendix B: Sample Book for Beginners

Appendix C: Sample Research Project Outline

Title:
Description:
Food:
Different Species:
Enemies:
Habitat:
Reproduction:
Special Features:

Contributor

Esperanza Saludes Jacobson teaches at Hampton Street Elementary School, Mineola, New York, in the United States.

Ready to Go

Levels
Beginning

Aims
Prepare for formal
alphabetic keyboarding
lessons with a software
program
Learn basic verbs and
sequence words

Class Time
20–30 minutes daily for
2 months

Resources
Items of computer
hardware and software
at various times in class
(e.g., keyboard only,
disks only)

Contributor

Procedure

1. Write a letter to parents explaining the language benefits of a keyboarding program.
2. Test students' handwriting rates (words per minute) in their native languages and writing systems.
3. Teach the following verbs using Total Physical Response: *press, place, stretch, go back, put in, take out, strike, reach, repeat, type, sit back*. Also teach the expression *supposed to*.
4. Reinforce the verbs using the computer items you have in class that day: "Press the *f* key," "reach for the *g* key," "first turn on the monitor."
5. Follow up with reading activities using the verbs studied.
6. Continue this procedure until the students' typing speed equals their handwriting rate.

Caveats and Options

This activity can provide remedial computer training in a sheltered haven.

Jacqueline Leigh is a librarian and ESL teacher at the American International School of Freetown, Sierra Leone.

Part XIII: Dice and Board Games

Andrew Thi-Ha at Kings Park Elementary School, Burke, Virginia, USA.

Vocabulary Dice Game

Levels
Beginning–low
intermediate

Aims
Practice vocabulary
(e.g., numbers, days of
the week, months,
colors, names of
classmates, furniture)
Be creative
Play cooperatively and
noncompetitively

Class Time
15–40 minutes

Resources
Poster-sized game board
Smaller game boards
and dice pairs for each
group of students
Crayons or markers

Procedure

1. Prepare several copies of a game board, including a poster-sized one for demonstration. (See Appendix.) Display the large game board at the front of the class.
2. Explain that the object of the game is to color in the game board and that players proceed by rolling dice, counting the appropriate number of spaces (in English), and coloring each space they land on.
3. Demonstrate one player's turn as follows:
   - Choose a space to start on and color it in.
   - Roll the dice and count off the correct number of spaces by saying numbers, days of the week, months, or other vocabulary, one word per space.
   - Color the space you land on.
4. Demonstrate two or three more turns, using a different color each time to indicate that you are a different player.
5. Divide the class into groups of three to five students. Give each group a game board and crayons. Have each group member choose a different color, decide which space to start at, and color in that space.
6. Have the students take turns rolling the dice. The one with the highest number gets to go first, starting from the space she or he colored in. On each turn, the students start from the last space they colored in. Because the object of the game is to color in the board, students should help other group members who get stuck or skip a word.
7. End the game when all of the spaces are colored in or when the available time is up.

Caveats and Options

1. Making the game boards as irregular as possible, with spaces that are all different shapes and sizes, makes the game more interesting and unusual, helps the children to avoid focusing on winning and losing, and demonstrates that things don't have to be exactly equal all the time.

2. You may wish to indicate that, if the dice go off the board, the player who rolled loses a turn. This helps children learn to be careful with the dice.

3. This game can be used to practice a wider range of vocabulary by including a set of category cards (e.g., furniture, food, parts of the body, pets) with each game board. For each turn, players roll the dice, pick a card, and say words from that category as they move over the spaces.

4. If your students are extreme beginners, have them use just one die to play the game.

5. To make the game boards reusable, laminate them and have the students color them with water-soluble pens.

Appendix: Sample Game Board

Contributor

Nat Caulk is a doctoral student at the University of Marburg in Germany.

Preposition Games With Pictures

Levels
Beginning–low
intermediate

Aims
Practice using
prepositions in an
enjoyable way

Class Time
15–20 minutes

Resources
Large picture with many
and varied items (e.g.,
people at work, children
playing in a park, a farm
scene)
Set of preposition cards
Tokens (e.g., plastic
discs, seeds, stones,
coins)
One die

Procedure

1. Draw clearly marked squares on the picture and photocopy it for each group in your class.
2. Prepare a set of cards with one preposition on each. Place them in a box.
3. Divide the class into small groups, not more than six students per group. Distribute the photocopied pictures.
4. Let children decide where the game should end (e.g., top right square).
5. Have the children place their tokens on either the bottom left-hand or bottom right-hand corner of the board and take turns throwing the die and moving the number of spaces shown.
6. When a player lands on a square, have him or her draw a card or slip of paper and use the preposition to move to a different square. For example, if a player lands on the square where there is a boy and draws a card that reads *over*, the player moves *over* the boy.

Contributor

Hyacinth Gaudart teaches at the University of Malaya, Kuala Lumpur, Malaysia.

Vocabulary Relay

Levels
Any

Aims
Practice and review
vocabulary and/or
simple sentence
patterns
Use numbers for
communicative
purposes

Class Time
15–20 minutes

Resources
30 flash cards with
words, pictures, or both
that the students have
already learned
Two dice

Procedure

1. Lay the cards face up in a long line on the floor or on desks, depending on the available space.
2. Divide the students into two teams. Have the teams line up behind either end of the line of flash cards.
3. Give one die to the first student on each team. Tell these two students to walk along the line of cards toward each other, pointing to each card in turn and reading the word or naming the picture aloud. If a student does not know a word or makes a mistake, have the student return to the back of the line and give the die to the next person on his or her team.
4. Continue until two students from opposing teams meet at a flash card. At this point, let the two players roll their dice. Allow the player who rolls the higher number to continue. The other player must return to the back of the line, passing the turn and the die to the next person on his or her team.
5. End the activity when one person reaches the opposite end of the line of flash cards. When a student does this, declare his or her team the winner.

Caveats and Options

1. This activity can also be used to review simple sentence patterns (e.g., *I'm hungry. I would like some* _____. *I'm thirsty. I would like some* _____.). Use flash cards with food and drink items and instruct the students to reproduce the correct sentence structure for each card, rather than simply saying the name of the item.
2. This activity can also be used to review the alphabet and numbers.

3. Students enjoy this very lively and energetic classroom activity partly because of the chance factor involved in rolling the dice. If you allow the team members to prompt each other, you will achieve the valuable asset of student correction in the classroom.
4. The optimum team size is five or six students. If you have a large class, consider using two lines of flash cards and four teams.

Contributor

Jason D. Halstead teaches at the Language Academy, Maebashi, Gunma, Japan.

Verb Tense Dice

Levels
High beginning–
intermediate

Aims
Actively review and
practice basic verb
tenses

Class Time
15–25 minutes

Resources
Blackboard
One die

Procedure

1. Write the following on the blackboard:
   1 = Now (present continuous)
   2 = Yesterday (past)
   3 = Every day (present)
   4 = Going to (future)
   5 = Will (future)
   6 = Choice
   Also write one common verb that the class has mastered.
2. Have the children roll the die in turn.
3. Ask the active roller to make a sentence in the tense that corresponds to the number rolled on the die and to use the time expression indicated. If a child rolls a 6, the child may choose which tense he or she wants to use. The roller must use the verb written on the blackboard in the sentence.
4. When all of the children have had one roll, change the verb on the blackboard.

Caveats and Options

For a competitive version of this game, divide the class into two teams and award 1 point for every correct sentence. In this version, the number 6, *choice*, should be changed to *bonus*. The child who rolls a 6 continues to roll. If the next number is not a 6, the student must make a correct sentence using the tense that the number represents. A correct answer receives an additional point for each 6 rolled. The first team to make 10 points is the winner.

Contributors

Peter Hastorf and Arlene Orensky teach at the Taipei American School, Taiwan, Republic of China.

Trees and Waterfalls

Levels
Any

Aims
Recognize numbers,
colors, and pictures
Recognize words
Form declarative and
interrogative sentences
Other, depending on
which game sheet is
used

Class Time
15 minutes

Resources
Hard plastic game cover
(see Appendix)
Game sheets (see
Appendix)
One die
Different playing piece
for each student
Spinner with sentence-
type selectors
(optional—see
Appendix)
Vocabulary cards
containing pictures,
words, or both
(optional)

Procedure

1. Seat the children around a small table or on the floor.
2. Select a game sheet and put it under the plastic game cover.
3. Have the children take turns rolling the die, moving their playing pieces, and performing activities related to the squares they land on. (Example: Using the numbers game sheet, children must say the numbers they land on in English. More advanced students could make up a sentence or phrase using the number.)
4. If a child lands on a space at the bottom of a tree, he or she immediately "climbs" to the top of the tree. If a child lands on a space at the top of a waterfall, he or she immediately "slides" to the bottom of the waterfall.
5. The first child to reach the Finish square is the winner.

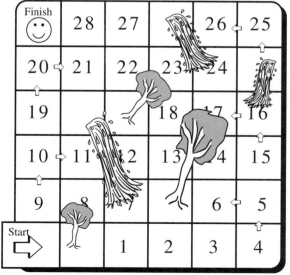

141

Caveats and Options

1. This activity works best with small groups of children.
2. Use vocabulary cards, realia, or a spinner to provide variety. (For example, advanced students can roll the die, move to the correct space, then use the spinner to determine what type of sentence to make.)
3. To make the activity less competitive, have students answer in unison whenever a player lands on a square.
4. To make the activity more competitive, have students lose a turn for incorrect answers.
5. To make the game longer, require students to roll the exact number to land on the Finish square. If they roll a number that is too high, they must move backward for the excess and risk landing on a waterfall.

Appendix: Sample Game Cover, Game Sheets, and Optional Spinner

Plastic Game Cover

Game Sheet:
be + -ing

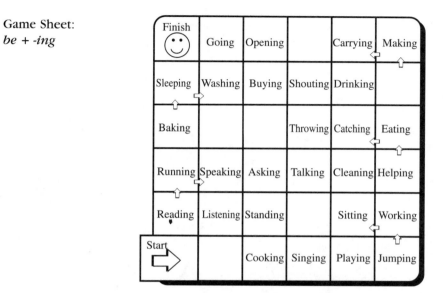

Game Sheet Inside Cover: Pictures

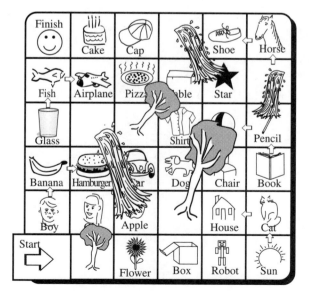

Optional Spinner

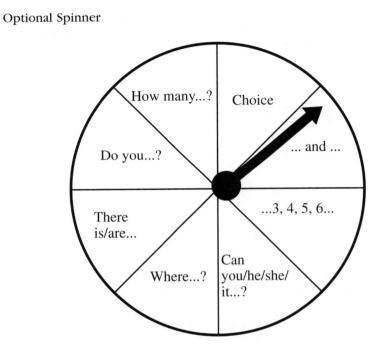

Contributor

Richard Humphries teaches at Kansai Gaidai College, Osaka, Japan.

Racetrack Game

Levels
Any

Aims
Practice identifying
pictures
Practice defining words
or using words in
sentences

Class Time
15–20 minutes

Resources
Game board(s) (see
Appendix)
One or more sets of
cards containing
pictures to identify (e.g.,
animals, holiday
symbols, articles of
clothing) or words to
define or use in a
sentence
Different colored
playing pieces
One die

Procedure

1. Seat three to five children around a game board on which a set of cards is placed face down.
2. Have each child choose a playing piece and place it at the starting line.
3. Let the children take turns rolling the die, picking up the top card, and responding to the card. (See Caveats and Options.) If a child responds to a card correctly, he or she moves ahead the number of spaces indicated on the die (and follows any instructions on the space he or she lands on). If a child responds incorrectly, he or she does not move.
4. As the cards are used, have the children place them face down at the bottom of the deck.
5. End the game when all the players reach home.

Caveats and Options

To shorten the playing time, use two dice or a die with large numbers.

Appendix: Game Board

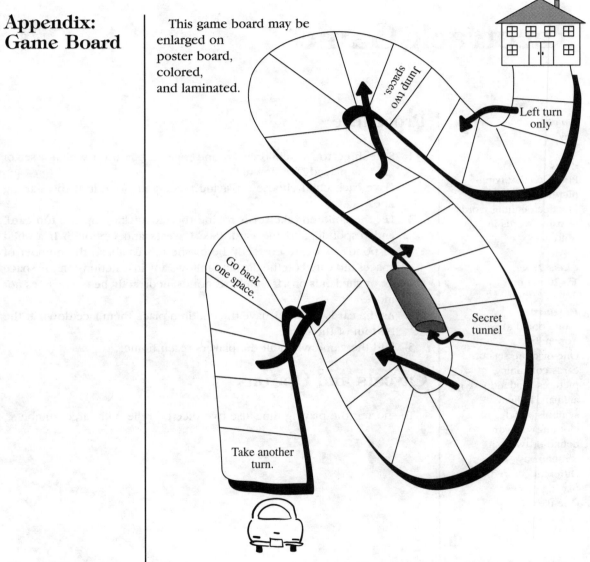

This game board may be enlarged on poster board, colored, and laminated.

Jump two spaces.

Left turn only

Go back one space.

Secret tunnel

Take another turn.

Contributor

Victoria Marone teaches in the Milwaukee Public Schools, Milwaukee, Wisconsin, in the United States.

Baseball Game

Levels
Any

Aims
Practice pronunciation
of vocabulary words
studied
Practice spelling of
vocabulary words
studied

Class Time
Minimum of 10-15
minutes

Resources
Large baseball diamond
(36 in. by 36 in. is a
good size) drawn on
heavy paper with bases
marked and scoring
indicated (see Step 7)
Picture cards of
vocabulary words
One die
Four counters (e.g.,
buttons, coins, or
magnets)
Paper and pencil

Contributor

Procedure

1. Divide children into two teams. Choose team names. One team pitches; they will ask questions. The other team goes up to bat; they will answer questions.
2. Have a pitching team member draw a card, hold it up, and ask, "What is it?" Have the batter answer, "It's a _____."
3. If the batter answers correctly, have the pitcher ask, "How do you spell it?" Ask the batter to reply.
4. If the batter answers correctly, have him or her roll the die. If the batter does not know the answer, he or she should say, "I don't know" and receive one strike. An incorrect answer is also one strike.
5. Let the batter play until he or she gets three strikes; then that player is out, and another player bats.
6. Continue to play until the batting team has three outs; then they pitch while the other team bats.
7. Keep score, or have a student keep score. (Die = 1, the batter moves her counter to first base; 2, to second base; 3, to third base; 4, to home; 5 is a ball; and 6 is a strike.)
8. Continue play for as many innings or runs as you like.

Caveats and Options

1. Keep track of scores and play a class "Series."
2. Game cards can also contain *wh-* questions, questions calling for personal responses, questions reviewing content material, or commands.

Linda Wells is a master's student at Temple University Japan in Osaka.

Part XIV: Card and Other Games

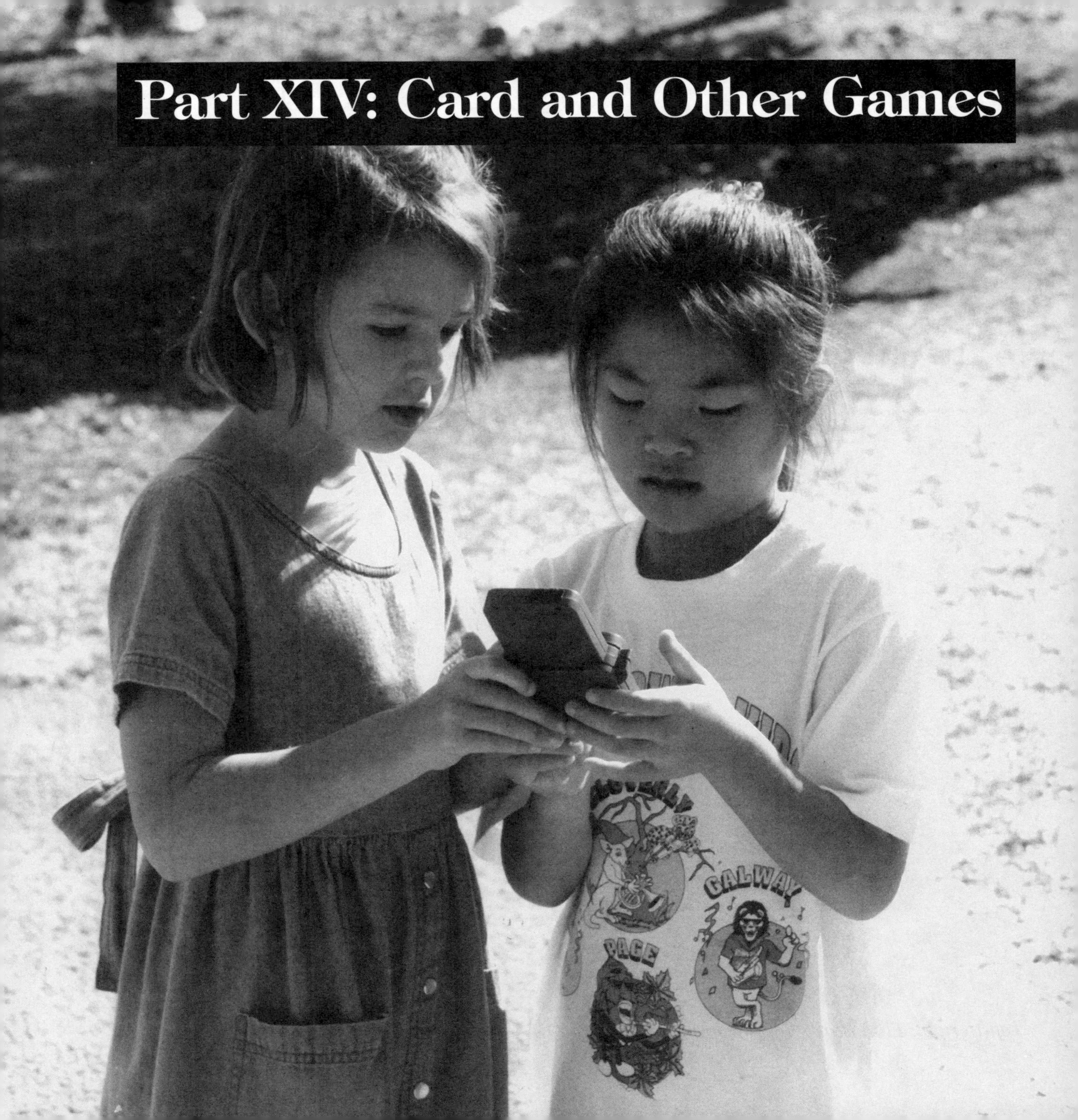

Left to right: Elise Barth and Meena Na at Kings Park Elementary School, Burke, Virginia, USA.

Adjective Rummy

Levels
Beginning

Aims
Practice reading,
speaking, and
understanding common
adjectives used to
describe feelings

Class Time
15–30 minutes

Resources
40 index cards with
adjectives printed on
one side (one set for
each group of four or
five students)

Procedure

1. Before the game, choose 10 adjectives that describe feelings (e.g., *happy*, *sad*, *tired*, *worried*, *energetic*, *excited*, *joyful*).
2. Print each adjective on four different cards.
3. Divide the class into groups of four or five. Give each group a set of cards.
4. Shuffle the cards and deal five to each child. Place the remaining cards facedown in the center of the group.
5. Tell Player 1 to ask another player in his or her group a question, such as "Rosa, do you feel tired?"
6. If Rosa has one or more cards that say *tired*, have her give one to Player 1 and say, "Yes, I feel tired." If Rosa does not have a *tired* card, she should reply, "No, I don't feel tired."
7. If Player 1 receives a card and a favorable reply, have that player continue to ask other group members until every player has been asked or until someone replies "No . . . ." Then have the next player to the right take a turn.
8. If a player receives a negative reply to his or her first question, have that child draw a card from the deck. The turn then passes to the next player on the right.
9. Declare the first player to lay down all of his or her cards the winner. There are two ways to lay down cards:
   - Lay down groups of three matching cards. (This may be done at any time.)
   - Lay a matching card down on your own or someone else's group of three.

151

Caveats and Options

Let the children think up their own set of adjectives related to a topic such as the weather, the school, or your city.

Contributor

Mark N. Brock teaches at the City University of Hong Kong.

Wh- Game

Levels
Intermediate +

Aims
Practice making *wh-*
questions with modals,
to be verbs, and other
verbs

Class Time
45–60 minutes or a full
class period

Resources
28-in. by 22-in. game
board and 30 value
cards (see Appendix)
30 answer cards
Chart with list of 20
verbs: *is, am, are, was,
were, do, does, did, can,
could, will, would,
shall, should, have, has,
had, may, might, must*

Procedure

1. The *Wh-* Game is played like the television game *Jeopardy*. Make 30 answer cards, 5 of which are answers to *who* questions, 5 of which are answers to *what* questions, and so on. Answers with values of 5 are the easiest, and those with values of 25 are the most difficult. For example, the answer under *who* for 5 might be *your grandmother*, and a possible question would be *Who is married to your grandfather?* The answer under *who* for 25 might be *George Washington*, and a possible question might be *Who was the first president of the United States?*

2. Place the game board at the front of the classroom. Place the verb chart next to it for reference.

3. Have each student take a turn by requesting a column and a value (e.g., "I'll take *who* for 25.").

4. Have the student read the answer and create a question using the *wh-* word at the head of the column to match the answer.

5. If the student creates a logical and grammatically correct question using one of the verbs listed, allow him or her to keep the value card and go on to the next student.

6. After questions have been provided for all of the answers, have the students total their value cards. The student who has the highest total value of cards is the winner.

Appendix: Game Board

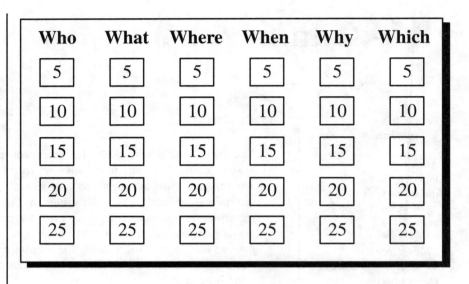

Who	What	Where	When	Why	Which
5	5	5	5	5	5
10	10	10	10	10	10
15	15	15	15	15	15
20	20	20	20	20	20
25	25	25	25	25	25

Contributor

Doris Clark teaches at Manheim Township Middle School, Lancaster, Pennsylvania, in the United States.

Linking Game

Levels
Beginning–intermediate

Aims
Practice new
grammatical structures
Check comprehension

Class Time
15–30 minutes

Resources
Envelopes
Four sentences cut into
component parts for
each envelope

Procedure

1. Divide the class into groups with not more than four members in each.
2. Give out one envelope per group.
3. Give the groups 15–30 minutes to compose a complete sentence from the components in the envelope. Each group member must compose a different sentence.
4. Have each group read its sentences as the students check them all together.
5. After playing the game, have the students write all the sentences they can find in their notebooks.

Caveats and Options

This activity is noncompetitive, but you may wish to give a point for every correct sentence.

Teresa Deagostini teaches at Colegio Jean Piaget and Crandon Institute, Montevideo, Uruguay.

Contributor

Matching Questions and Answers

Levels
Beginning

Aims
Practice reading
Demonstrate listening
comprehension
Practice pronunciation
of words already learned

Class Time
10-15 minutes

Resources
Cards containing
questions (one question
per card)
Cards containing
corresponding answers
(one answer per card)

Procedure

1. Seat the children in a circle.
2. Divide the class into two groups, A and B.
3. Give each group half the question cards. Spread out the answer cards in the middle of the circle.
4. Have one student from Group A read a question aloud. Ask the students in Group B to look for the answer. When they find it, one student must read it aloud.
5. Continue in this manner, with the groups taking turns asking and answering questions, until every question has been asked and correctly answered.

Caveats and Options

1. If you like, give each group 1 point for every correct answer. If you prefer a noncompetitive activity, simply collect both cards after a question is answered correctly.
2. To practice writing and reinforce acquired knowledge, have the members of both groups copy the questions and answers on paper.

Teresa Deagostini teaches at Colegio Jean Piaget and Crandon Institute, Montevideo, Uruguay.

Contributor

My Mother Went to the Supermarket

Levels
Beginning–intermediate

Aims
Practice the past tense
Practice saying and remembering the names of items found in a supermarket

Class Time
10–15 minutes

Resources
None

Contributor

Procedure

1. Have one child start by saying, "My mother went to the supermarket and she bought a [any supermarket item]."
2. Ask another child to continue by repeating what the first child said and adding another item.
3. Continue around the room, with each child repeating the list thus far and adding an item to it.
4. When a child makes a mistake, he or she is out and the next child starts a new list. The winner is the last remaining player.

Caveats and Options

This is an ideal whole-class activity.

Richard Jacobs is an independent EFL consultant.

What Am I?

Levels
Any

Aims
Practice asking and
answering questions
Practice using
descriptive language
Reinforce concept area
vocabulary

Class Time
20 minutes

Resources
Picture cards or word
cards
Masking tape

Caveats and Options

Contributor

Procedure

1. Seat the children so that all may see you.
2. Briefly review all the cards with the class. All the cards should contain pictures or words from one general category and, ideally, relate to a theme, unit, or content area currently being studied. For example, pictures of a lighthouse, beach, octopus, fish, whale, and boat would be appropriate for primary students currently using the ocean as a theme in a whole language classroom. Vocabulary words from a chapter of a science textbook could be used with older students who are more advanced in English.
3. Have the students choose (without your knowledge) a card and affix it to your back with masking tape. Model the type of questions you wish to introduce or reinforce until you have the necessary information; then guess who you are. Examples are *Am I an animal? Do I have fins?* and so on.
4. Choose a student to follow your lead. Continue the game until all students have participated.

Specify particular question types to be used, such as *wh-* questions or *yes/no* questions.

Linda Allison LaVelle is a language specialist in the Federal Hocking Local Schools, Coolville, Ohio, in the United States.

What's His Name?

Levels
Beginning (basic reading skills required)

Aims
Review simple present-tense questions in the first and third person

Class Time
30 minutes

Resources
10–15 pairs of cue cards containing first-person questions and answers (see Appendix A)
Worksheet with corresponding third-person questions (see Appendix B)

Procedure

Part 1

1. Place the cue cards facedown on a table in a random arrangement. The question cards and answer cards should be separated into two groups.
2. Demonstrate to the students that the object of the activity is to find the matching pairs of questions and answers:
   - Select a question card and read it aloud.
   - Choose an answer card in an attempt to find the appropriate reply.
   - If you select the correct answer, keep the pair and take a second turn. Put an incorrect pair back on the table facedown.
3. Have the students take turns selecting question cards and attempting to find the correct answers.
4. End the game when all the question-and-answer pairs have been identified. The student who has the most cards is the winner.

Part 2

1. Place the corresponding question-and-answer pairs face up on the table. Repeat the questions to the students using the third person, and elicit the grammatically correct responses. Involve all the students in this activity with rapid-fire questions and repetition.
2. Put away the cue cards. Give each student a worksheet containing the third-person questions. Have the students ask each other the questions and complete their worksheets as a group activity.

Caveats and Options

When creating the cue cards, keep in mind that each question card must have only one possible answer card. Likewise, each answer card must go with only one question card.

Appendix A: Sample Cue Card Questions and Answers

What's your name?	My name is Roberto.
Where do you live?	I live in San Diego.
What country are you from?	I'm from Spain.
What nationality are you?	I'm Spanish.
What's your occupation?	I'm a chef.
Where do you work?	At El Sol restaurant.
How many brothers and sisters do you have?	I have one brother and two sisters.
What are your hobbies?	I like playing soccer and listening to rock music.
What languages can you speak?	I can speak Spanish, English, and Portuguese.
Who's your favorite movie star?	I like the actress Julia Roberts.
What are your favorite foods?	Steak and fries!

Appendix B: Sample Worksheet With Third-Person Questions

Complete the questions and then number them in any order. Ask the questions to other students. How many of the answers can you and your classmates remember?

What's his name?
Where does he live?
What country ____ ____ from?
____ nationality is ____?
What's his occupation?
Where ____ ____ work?
____ ____ ____ and sisters does he have?
What ____ his hobbies?
What languages can he ____?
Who's his favorite movie star?
____ ____ his favorite foods?

Contributor

Claire E. J. Potter teaches at the Language Academy, Maebashi, Gunma, Japan.

Old Onion

Levels
Beginning

Aims
Reinforce names of
foods
Practice pronunciation
of food words

Class Time
10–30 minutes,
depending on the
number of players and
the number of
vocabulary cards

Resources
3-in. by 5-in. index cards
Two pictures of each
food taught
One picture of an onion

Procedure

1. Before class, paste each picture onto an index card. Laminate the cards if possible.
2. In class, deal out all the cards.
3. Let the students take turns identifying pairs in their hands, naming them, and discarding them onto a pile in the center of the playing area.
4. Let each player, in turn, pick one card from the hand of the player on his or her right. If the card matches one he or she holds, the pair is shown, named, and discarded.
5. Continue playing until one person is left with only one card—the onion! He or she is the Old Onion— the loser (or the winner)!

Caveats and Options

This game can be played with any pairs of related pictures plus one odd one, such as nouns (clothing, furniture, colors and shapes, animals), numbers, and phonic pairs (beginning, medial, and final sounds).

Helene Linet Stone is a retired ESL and bilingual director/teacher living in Highwood, Illinois, in the United States.

Contributor

What's Missing?

Levels
Any

Aims
Elicit verbal responses
of varying lengths
(depending on student
proficiency) in a
gamelike atmosphere

Class Time
5–10 minutes

Resources
Cards with pictures of
previously studied
vocabulary

Procedure

1. Lay the picture cards face up on a table or on the chalkboard ledge.
2. Tell the students to close their eyes. While their eyes are closed, remove one card.
3. Tell the students to open their eyes. Ask, "What's missing?"
4. The first student to respond correctly becomes the next "teacher." He or she repeats Steps 2 and 3.

Caveats and Options

1. If you have a large number of picture cards available, remove one or two cards and replace them with new cards after each round.
2. Depending on the students' proficiency level, use this activity for more than merely vocabulary review. A beginning-level response might be simple noun identification: *the car* (versus *the horse*) or *a car* (versus *the car*). A higher beginning-level response might be *the green car* (versus *the red car*). An intermediate-level response might be *the car with the broken window* (versus *the car with the flat tire*). An advanced-level response might be *the car that costs $8,000* (versus *the car that has a broken window*). The appropriate answers will, of course, depend on the picture cards used and the structures already practiced in class.
3. Use an overhead projector and a transparency containing the appropriate pictures instead of the picture cards. In this version, there is no need to have the children close and open their eyes. Simply switch off

the projector, black out one item with a small piece of paper, and turn the projector on again.

4. Divide the class into teams and conduct this as a competitive activity.

Contributor

Carl Watts teaches at Boise State University, Boise, Idaho, in the United States.

Also available from TESOL

All Things to All People
Donald C. Flemming, Lucie C. Germer, and Christiane Kelley

Books for a Small Planet:
An Intercultural Bibliography for Young English Language Learners
Dorothy S. Brown

Common Threads of Practice:
Teaching English to Children Around the World
Katharine Davies Samway and Denise McKeon, Editors

Dialogue Journal Writing with Nonnative English Speakers:
A Handbook for Teachers
Joy Kreeft Peyton and Leslee Reed

Dialogue Journal Writing with Nonnative English Speakers:
An Instructional Packet for Teachers and Workshop Leaders
Joy Kreeft Peyton and Jana Staton

Diversity as Resource:
Redefining Cultural Literacy
Denise E. Murray, Editor

E-Mail for English Teaching:
Bringing the Internet and Computer Learning Networks Into the
Language Classroom
Mark Warschauer

New Ways in Teacher Education
Donald Freeman, with Steve Cornwell, Editors

New Ways in Teaching Reading
Richard R. Day, Editor

New Ways in Teaching Speaking
Kathleen M. Bailey and Lance Savage, Editors

New Ways in Teaching Writing
Ronald V. White, Editor

Video in Second Language Teaching:
Using, Selecting, and Producing Video for the Classroom
Susan Stempleski and Paul Arcario, Editors

For more information, contact

Teachers of English to Speakers of Other Languages, Inc.
1600 Cameron Street, Suite 300
Alexandria, Virginia 22314 USA
Tel 703-836-0774 • Fax 703-836-7864